OVER THE IVY WALLS

SUNY Series, Social Context of Education
Christine E. Sleeter, Editor

OVER THE IVY WALLS

The Educational Mobility of Low-Income Chicanos

Patricia Gándara

STATE UNIVERSITY OF NEW YORK PRESS

Published by
State University of New York Press, Albany

© 1995 State University of New York

For information, address State University of New York Press,
State University Plaza, Albany, N.Y., 12246

Production by Cathleen Collins
Marketing by Dana Yanulavich

Library of Congress Cataloging in Publication Data

Gándara, Patricia C.
    Over the ivy walls : the educational mobility of low-income
Chicanos / Patricia Gándara.
        p.   cm. — (SUNY series, social context of education)
    Includes bibliographical references and index.
    ISBN 0-7914-2609-2. — ISBN 0-7914-2610-6 (pbk.)
    1. Mexican Americans—Education (Higher)—Social aspects.
    2. Mexican Americans—Education (Higher)—Economic aspects.
    3. Academic achievement—United States.   4. Educational sociology—
United States.   I. Title. II. Series.
    LC2683.6.G36   1995
    371.97'6872073—dc20   94-38546
                                                                            CIP

10 9 8 7 6 5 4 3 2 1

Contents

Tables

Acknowledgments

This book could not have been written without the willing and generous cooperation of the people whose lives are recounted in the following pages. I will be forever grateful for their candid and perceptive accounts, as well as for their inspiration. When time limitations and competing demands threatened to abort this project, rereading passages from these most extraordinary lives always renewed my resolve that these stories must be told. Thus the subjects provided not only the major content of the book, but also the impetus for its creation. What they said, and the enormously articulate ways in which they said it, was simply too compelling to leave in a file cabinet.

These are all pioneers of a new professional and academic élite. Unlike their predecessors, and most of their colleagues, the mantle did not pass naturally from the shoulders of one generation to the next, nor does it always rest easily, even now. Rather, these people had to build an understanding of what it meant to be an intellectual or professional without benefit of inheritance. They have transcended the fields and the barrios to become academics—dispensers and creators of knowledge—in a culture that more often views them as ignorant; doctors and lawyers—representatives of the most prestigious occupations—in a world that views them as powerless. These were not easy transitions, nor were they always easily recounted; more than a few tears were shed in the telling.

I also gratefully acknowledge the financial support of a number of "patrons": RAND Corporation for initial seed money; the California Policy Seminar which provided for completion of the major data collection and transcription; the Chicana/Latina Research Center of the University of California at Davis, and Eugene Garcia and the Latino Eligibility Study, for helping to fund data collection on women; and the University of California at Davis, for precious time to complete the manuscript. Each contributed critically to the final product, though none bears any responsibility for what has been written; any blame lies solely with the author.

Preface

The idea for this book began many years ago and grew out of the author's experiences working as a school psychologist in low-income, all-minority schools in Los Angeles. Students who are referred to the school psychologist there are often those on whom teachers have given up. These are the students "at risk" for school failure who are in the process of dropping out, if not physically, then at least mentally and emotionally. Typically, the students I saw were from homes where families were stressed to the breaking point by poverty, low skills, ignorance of the English language, and lack of opportunity. These students' schools were ill-equipped to address their needs, and they were alienated from the schooling experience; they were just "putting in their time." Sadly, there was little I could do as a psychologist to change the reality of their situations.

Yet, every once in a while, from this same desperate environment, I would see a student for whom schooling was a redeeming experience: a student whose parents did not have as much as an elementary school education, but who was dedicated to learning; who never heard a word of English spoken at home, but who excelled in language arts; who had heavy responsibilities at home, but always completed the homework assignments. These students were referred to me because they were believed by their teachers to be "gifted."

The question continued to nag at me, long after I left that job and embarked on a career as a researcher and teacher: What caused those students who excelled in spite of these bleak circumstances to beat the odds? What would motivate some of them to go on to university educations? The simple answer has always been that these students were simply born more intellectually capable. Yet, anyone who has worked in the barrio, or in the ghetto, has seen many kids just as bright, and perhaps brighter, who take a very different path. As research has piled up over the years, detailing the formidable barriers faced by low-income Hispanic (Chicano) students in pursuing education, the question of what makes these kids different has become even more compelling. Our increased understanding of the factors that lead to failure has not appreciably diminished the rate of failure experienced by Chicano students. Perhaps a better understanding of what leads to academic success will yield more fruitful outcomes. This study, then, was an attempt to come to a better understanding of the forces that push some Chicano students, born and raised in environments that typically yield academic failure, over the ivy walls of academia, and into the highest status professions.

Introduction

This is a study of high academic achievement found in the most unlikely of places: among low-income Mexican Americans from homes with little formal education. It is an examination of the forces that conspire to create such anomalies, and its aim is to suggest how such outcomes might be the product of design rather than of accident.

THE CONTEXT OF EDUCATION FOR HISPANICS

Hispanics[1] are the least educated major population group in the United States (Chapa, 1991). They are the least likely to graduate from high school, enroll in college, and receive a college degree (Carter & Wilson, 1993). For example, in California and Texas, where more than one-third of the college-age population is Hispanic, only 11 to 13 percent are enrolled in four-year colleges. Even so, substantially fewer than half of these students can be expected to complete an undergraduate degree within six years of having commenced their studies (Aguirre & Martinez, 1993).

The disproportionately low representation of Hispanics in higher education throughout the nation is the product of several circumstances: extremely high drop-out rates before high school graduation, inadequate preparation for continued study, and the tendency for many college-eligible Hispanics to eschew four-year institutions (California Postsecondary Education Commission, 1986; Rumberger, 1991). Most Hispanic students who do commit to

---

1. "Hispanic" refers to the Bureau of the Census term for people who originate from Spanish-speaking countries. This term is used to reference data that are collected and reported for all Hispanic groups combined. In the United States, Mexican origin people comprise the largest Hispanic subgroup, followed by Puerto Ricans, Cubans, and Central and South Americans. A very small percentage of Hispanics trace their direct origins to Spain.

postsecondary education begin and end their college careers in two-year institutions without obtaining a degree. Transfer rates from two-year institutions to four-year colleges and universities are notoriously low for Hispanic students, with as few as 6 percent actually making the shift (Rendon & Nora, 1989). The reasons cited for the heavy student attrition at this point range from the inability to continue foregoing earnings while attending school to a failure to integrate into the life and routines of the college campus (Aguirre & Martinez, 1993). Whatever the reasons, and there appear to be many, the overwhelming majority of Hispanic students who opt for a postsecondary education do not achieve their aims of acquiring a college degree, and quickly find themselves on the job market, unskilled and undereducated.

This low level of education for Hispanics is related to their poor performance in the American economy, with nearly 40 percent of Hispanic children living in poverty (Chapa, 1991). Given that 10 percent of the nation's labor force will be Hispanic by the year 2000, their undereducation portends potentially grave consequences for the economy and social structure of the United States, and especially the American Southwest where most Hispanics reside and where they comprise the largest single population group in a number of urban areas.

This study focuses on the educational mobility of one Hispanic group, the most numerous: Mexican Americans or Chicanos.[2] Already established in the American Southwest before the territory was ceded to the United States, Chicanos have a legacy distinct from other Hispanics, which has resulted in different patterns of opportunity and achievement. Of all the Hispanic groups, Mexican Americans experience the greatest educational risk (De La Rosa & Maw, 1990), making their situation all the more urgent.

Whether the educational situation has been improving or deteriorating for Chicano students over the past several years remains a debatable issue. One measure of academic progress is statewide achievement test scores. Between 1987 and 1990, results from the California Assessment program (CAP) showed a widening in the gap between the scores of Hispanics and those for the state as a whole (Policy Analysis for California Education, 1991). McCarthy and Valdez (1986), however, have contended that the number of years of education completed by Mexican Americans increases substantially with each successive generation, and that educational statistics can be misleading because of high levels of immigration of poor and undereducated Mexican nationals. On the other hand, Chapa (1991) has compared the rates of

---

2. Throughout the book, Mexican American and Chicano are used interchangeably to denote the same population: residents of the United States who are of Mexican origin. Nationwide, they comprise more than 60 percent of all Hispanics, and in California and Texas they represent more than 80 percent of the Hispanic population.

immigration against trends in achievement and has concluded that the data do not support the argument that high levels of immigration explain the achievement gap between Mexican Americans and non-Hispanic whites. He asserts that a phenomenon of "educational stagnation" is occurring among Mexican American youth (Chapa & Valencia, 1993). Whether or not things are improving for Mexican Americans in school generally, there is widespread agreement that a ceiling remains on college-going behavior which has not yielded substantially to various intervention strategies (Gándara, 1986a; McCarthy & Valdez, 1986).

Although education is not the only road to social mobility, it has become increasingly important as the primary avenue into the middle class for underrepresented groups. Meanwhile, "qualifications inflation" has placed more and more jobs out of the reach of individuals who lack the appropriate academic credentials (Rumberger, 1981; McCarthy & Valdez, 1986). For example, of the new jobs being created through the year 2000, the Hudson Institute projects that 30 percent will require a college education, up from 22 percent of all jobs as recently as 1988 (Castle, 1993). In areas where a large percentage of the student population is Mexican American, the persistent underachievement of this group constitutes a serious mismatch between the needs of the economy and the skills and preparation of a substantial segment of the population. Moreover, it has become abundantly clear that real education reform and improvement will remain illusory until all population groups can be drawn into the mainstream of educational achievement. How to meet this challenge, however, continues to be an unanswered question for education policymakers.

RESEARCH ON CHICANO SCHOOL FAILURE

Since the 1960s, when specific data began to be collected on Mexican American school performance, a host of studies have focused on the causes of school failure for Chicanos. The logic that has guided these studies is that by understanding why students fail, changes can be made in the system, or the students, that will result in improved educational outcomes. The literature on Chicano school failure can be described as having evolved through several stages, roughly paralleling the previous three decades.

The decade of the 1960s, which saw the most impressive gains in history of civil rights for minorities, was one in which the scholarly literature focused on deprivation theories and ways to ameliorate this disadvantage. Minorities, such as Mexican Americans, were viewed as having fundamental deficits which schools and government could overcome through special interventions such as Headstart (Hess & Shipman, 1965; Valentine, 1968). As these efforts appeared to meet with only limited success, and failed to change the fundamental relationships of students to schools, the focus shifted in the 1970s to a cultural difference model.

The cultural difference model suggested that minorities were not so much "deprived" of important cultural experiences as they were participants in a different set of experiences that, while worthy in themselves, did not meet the expectations of schools (Carter & Segura, 1979; Buenning & Tollefson, 1987). One of the chief cultural differences between lower-income and middle-class students identified by researchers was speech style (Hymes, 1974). This focus on speech and language differences was especially salient for Chicanos because of the obvious differences between the language of the home and the language of school. Hence, this discontinuity in linguistic experience between home and school, coupled with other cultural differences came to explain academic failure. The major educational response to this theory of failure was bilingual/bicultural education.

Bilingual education has proved to be an important educational reform for many language minority groups, and particularly for Hispanics (Fernandez & Neilsen, 1986; Merino, 1991). It has established a template for providing limited-English-proficient (LEP) students with access to the core curriculum and has demonstrated that LEP students do not have to remain on the periphery of schooling until their English skills are sufficient to join the mainstream. Although the potential effect of bilingual education on long-term educational outcomes for Hispanic students has not been fully determined because of the very limited way in which this reform has been implemented and studied (Gándara & Sun, 1986), language differences apparently do not fully explain the achievement gap between Mexican Americans and others. Evidence for this lies in the fact that most Mexican Americans are English speakers, yet educational attainment for these students has remained low. As Nieto (1993) points out, "even with a bilingual education, many children are likely to face educational failure. . . . No approach or program can cure all problems, educational or otherwise, facing our young people if it does not also address the fundamental issues of discrimination and stratification in schools and society. . . . Simply substituting one language for another, or books in Spanish with Dick and Jane in brownface, will not guarantee success for language minority students. Expecting too much of even good programs is counterproductive because in the absence of quick results, the children are again blamed for their failures" (p. 205).

During this same time period, a parallel literature, whose greatest exponents were Samuel Bowles and Herbert Gintis (1976), had emerged to explain group differences in academic achievement as a function of capitalist economics. Discounted by most psychologists, the economic determinism of Bowles and Gintis's work found a home among those sociologists for whom such a model of social reproduction resonated with particular fervor. They contended that the schools functioned as a huge sorting mechanism in which ostensibly "meritocratic" criteria such as performance on standardized tests (on which white and middle- and upper-income children are known to out-perform their lower-income and minority peers) determine who shall be in the college-bound curriculum tracks and who shall remain in the lower cur-riculum tracks that do not prepare students for educational opportunities beyond high school. Such a seemingly fair system allows the schools to reproduce the class structure in a way that makes the students accept blame (once again) for their own failure: they aren't selected to be educated for the professions because they don't perform well enough. Bowles and Gintis, however, demonstrated quite convincingly that the relationship between ability test scores and distribution of opportunity is weak. Nonetheless, this supposedly meritocratic system serves to maintain the economic and social status quo. This was a theory that exposed the "hidden hand" of economic policy, yet it failed to explain differences among low-income and minority groups in their responses to the American school system, and the system's response to them.

As the strong bias in favor of quantitative methods of the 1970s began to give way in the 1980s to qualitative methods drawn from anthropology, more powerful and complex explanatory theories of minority school failure were introduced. This newer literature, which has focused on the social construction of disadvantage, has had the added benefit of being able to at least partially explain the variations among immigrant and minority groups and their relationship to educational systems. Ogbu (1987), and Ogbu and Matute-Bianchi (1986), have articulated a framework for studying minority school achievement which distinguishes between *immigrant minorities*, people who have come to the United States more or less voluntarily to seek greater oppor-tunity, and *involuntary* or *caste-like minorities*, those individuals who find themselves in the United States through slavery, conquest, or colonization. According to this framework, the immigrant minorities reference their situation in the United States to the homelands they fled, and in spite of discrimination and other barriers facing newcomers, find their present situation to be a hopeful one. On the other hand, the caste-like minorities mark as their reference point the members of their group who have already lived in the United States for generations and failed to secure a place within the main-stream. This results in an attitude of hopelessness and the adoption of behaviors that are defined in opposition to the practices and preferences of white Americans as a way of repudiating the negative stereotypes that are projected on them by the majority culture. Hence, if school achievement is a value of white culture, then doing well in school takes on the connotation of "acting white," anathema to the behavioral standards of the minority group. Ogbu and Matute-Bianchi have applied the framework specifically to Mexican Americans to explain the way in which group behaviors may both result from, and reinforce, majority-culture stereotypes that operate to maintain minority-group subordination.

Mehan (1992) and others (Cicourel & Mehan, 1985; Mehan, Hartweck & Meihls, 1986) likewise arguing for structural impediments to minority achievement, have suggested that bureaucratic school organization operates to maintain status differences between majority- and minority-culture students through what they call "constitutive rules." These are the rules of behavior and decision-making that determine the kind of curriculum to which children will be exposed. Low-income and minority students, because they come to school without the status characteristics of the middle and upper classes, are assigned to the lower tracks and groups in school where they can be "remediated." Higher status students are placed in the upper tracks and the faster reading groups where they can fulfill the prophecy of their more monied and educated heritage. In this way, the structure of the school promotes the idea among low-income and minority students that they cannot, and should not, compete with their social and academic superiors. Thus, these authors view the school as a perhaps unintentional, but nonetheless powerful, co-conspirator in society's reproduction of class differences. To the extent that some immigrant and other low-income students mirror the achievement characteristics of the middle and upper classes (e.g., adhering to the behavioral norms of the school, giving priority to studying over other kinds of activities), the bureaucratic structure of the schools can accommodate their mobility.

A somewhat different explanation of minority school failure has been offered by the "resistance" theorists. Giroux (1983), Willis (1977), and McLeod (1987) have invoked the notion of social agency in their explanations of school failure. Within this framework, the student is not seen as merely a pawn in an economic or bureaucratic structure, but as an active participant in deciding his or her own fate. Ironically, as in Willis's study of working-class "lads" who opt for working-class jobs, and McLeod's description of youth growing up in the housing projects who "choose" a future not unlike that of their parents, students' insights into their own circumstances, while often astute, are insufficient to allow them to break with their own cultural biases. Their resistance against what was perceived to be an unfair system often led them to reject opportunities to "make it" within that system. For Willis's lads, it was their identification of manual labor with male privilege which ensured the acceptance of their subordinate economic fate and the successful reproduction of class structure. Likewise, McLeod's "Hallway Hangers," in railing against a school system that they felt was biased against them, rejected the opportunities for skill development and socialization that might have led, at the least, to a life outside of prison. The perspective of the resistance theorists shares much with the writing of Ogbu on oppositional features of minority culture, yet it differs in the extent to which the resistance theorists focus on individual, as opposed to group, agency; the capacity of the individual to interpret his or her own circumstances and respond accordingly.

A third contemporary perspective on school failure has its roots in the work of Bourdieu and Passeron (1977), but has been elucidated in the North American context by Lareau (1987, 1989) and DiMaggio (1982). From this perspective, variation in school achievement can be traced to differences in cultural capital, defined as the general cultural background, knowledge, dispositions, and skills that are passed from one generation to another. Schools reward the cultural capital of the dominant classes and devalue that of the lower classes. Hence, as Lareau asserts in her study of working- and middle-class school communities, parents who understand and share the middle-class values of schools, are able to intervene on their children's behalf to assure that they benefit from all the school has to offer; lower-income and minority parents seldom share the same knowledge, dispositions, and skills to allow them to effect similar outcomes for their children.

DiMaggio (1982) studied the effect of students' appreciation for "high culture" (i.e., activities, attitudes, and information about art, literature, and music) on the grades they received in school. In a quantitative study, controlling for social class background, DiMaggio was able to demonstrate that cultural capital, defined in this way, did indeed influence classroom grades above and beyond the effect of parents' education. He hypothesized that because teachers are the greatest consumers of the arts, independent of socioeconomic status, they would be influenced positively by students who shared their dispositions, and in turn would view these students in a more positive light. While this study represents a more narrow construction of the notion of cultural capital than other researchers have construed, it nonetheless corroborates the assertion that information about, and ability to manipulate, the cultural forms of the middle and upper classes can be a significant asset to students, and one that is likely to be out of the reach of most low-income minority and immigrant children.

More recently, Portes and Zhou (1993) have suggested that "segmented assimilation" may account for the different adaptations of second generation minority children to American society and schooling. Drawing from a large data set of children of immigrants on both U.S. coasts, and augmented by the studies of Gibson (1987) with Punjabi children in Northern California and Matute-Bianchi (1986) with Mexican American and Japanese American children in California, Portes and Zhou conclude that rapid assimilation into American culture can have disastrous consequences for the children of immigrant minorities. Across the various immigrant groups, the most academically successful students were those who remained most closely allied with the culture of their parents. This seemingly paradoxical finding was explained in terms of group resources and attitudes. For Punjabi, Japanese, and Cuban American children, strong coethnic communities with considerable social and economic resources exist to reinforce the parental culture. These children find it relatively easy to accommodate the demands of school and American society without sacrificing the culture of the family or the authority structure that accompanies it. Hence, there is little dissonance in the demands and expectations of both school and family. For the children of Mexican and Haitian immigrants, on the other hand, the existence of large downtrodden coethnic communities can be worse than no community at all, because these children enter into ready contact with peers who have already established an oppositional subculture that rejects the values of their traditional families as well as of the school. In contrast, the children of Mexican immigrants who continued to refer to themselves as "Mexicano," as opposed to the referants "Chicano" or "Mexican American," and characterized themselves as more closely linked to the parental culture, were among the most successful in school. As Portes and Zhou note:

> Children of non-white immigrants may not even have the opportunity of gaining access to middle-class white society, no matter how acculturated they become. Joining those native circles to which they do have access may prove a ticket to permanent subordination and disadvantage. Remaining securely ensconced in their coethnic community, under these circumstances, may be not a symptom of escapism but the best strategy for capitalizing on otherwise unavailable material and moral resources . . . a strategy of paced, selective assimilation may prove the best course for immigrant minorities. (1993, p. 96)

Thus, Portes and Zhou, echoing, in part, the earlier work of Ogbu and Matute-Bianchi, locate the problem of chronic underachievement of Mexican American children within the structure of coethnic peer communities which absorb succeeding generations of Mexican origin children not into the mainstream but into an "adversarial stance of impoverished groups confined to the bottom of the new economic hourglass" (p. 85).

While new immigrants who are still tied to their native cultures often perform better in American schools even than those students who have been born in the United States (Portes & Rumbaut, 1994), most Chicano students have long since left behind the immigrant mentality that might have protected them from the competing force of an oppositional subculture (Macias, 1993). And ironically, though Chicano students also tend to have high academic and occupational *aspirations* (Portes & Rumbaut, 1993), in reality they quickly accommodate to the low levels of education and menial jobs that are the legacy of generations of Chicanos before them. To combat this reality, some researchers have suggested that the central strategy must be empowerment: empowering parents to advocate for their children (Delgado-Gaitan, 1990); empowering communities to change their schools (Trueba, 1988); and empowering students to reconceptualize their own self-image as learners (Gándara, 1992). Nonetheless, while the emerging literature suggests important insights into the cultural processes that contribute to underachievement, and some potential strategies for combatting it, it remains a literature with serious limitations.

Few studies seriously address the issue of *within-group* differences, that is, why some students, caught up in the same web of underachievement as their low-income, minority peers, reject that outcome. An important element missing from most of this research has been the insights which can be gained from an understanding of how students who don't fail, in spite of adverse circumstances, manage to escape that fate. With few exceptions (e.g., Gibson, 1987; Suarez-Orozco, 1987), the research has neglected to address this *other* compelling question. This book explores the characteristics and experiences of Chicanos who survive poverty and disadvantage to become highly successful academic achievers. In so doing, it also attempts to integrate some of the large body of research on academic achievement into a coherent understanding of how low-income Chicanos may find success in school. The pages that follow take a qualitative approach to the study of academic achievement in Chicanos. Hopefully, this approach yields new meanings and greater texture to the correlations, regressions, and theories that have been used to "explain" Chicano (under)achievement. In the subjects' own words, we explore how they came to deviate so extraordinarily from their pre-ordained paths and to boost themselves "over the ivy walls."

GOVERNMENT INTERVENTION IN THE
HIGHER EDUCATION OF CHICANOS

It was not until the 1960s, and the civil rights activities of that period, that government, either state or federal, paid much attention to the particular educational plight of Chicano students. However, historically there have been other attempts to support and stimulate higher-education attendance which no doubt have had an impact on Chicano students, however inadvertently. The best example of this was Public Law 346, known as the GI Bill, passed in 1944 on the heels of World War II. While the motives behind the legislation are variously described as being aimed at rehabilitating soldiers, avoiding massive unemployment and unrest, and supporting the growth of higher education (Olson, 1974; Henry, 1975), the bill afforded unprecedented opportunity to hundreds of thousands of working-class young men (and a few women) who would not have otherwise dreamed of a college education.[3] Into this category fell many Chicano war veterans who, in all probability, would have returned to the fields and the factories in which their parents worked had this extraordinary opportunity not presented itself. Instead, they formed a small but significant class of college- and university-educated Latino professionals. Unfortunately, data were not collected on the background characteristics of GI Bill recipients, hence our understanding of the impact of this phenomenon on Chicano participation in higher education remains anecdotal.

Not until the late 1950s and the 1960s was there another governmental initiative of similar magnitude that would aid the entry of "nontraditional" students into the ranks of academia. Financial aid and higher education recruitment programs, in the form of the National Defense Education Act (NDEA) of 1958 and the Higher Education Act of 1965, spurred the greatest increase in low-income and minority college student attendance in our history. Moreover, some private foundations, most notably the Ford Foundation, joined the effort with grants and fellowships directed at Mexican Americans who wished to pursue graduate education. Careful collection of data by ethnic and racial group has allowed us to follow the trends since that time. We know that, in spite of a social science literature that asserted that Chicanos were either incapable of, or disinterested in, higher education (Valencia, 1991), unprecedented numbers of Chicano students took advantage of the opportunities being offered, and by 1975 their rate of participation in higher education had peaked, and has not been matched since that time (Chapa, 1991).

---

3. The GI Bill provided up to 48 months of "full school costs, including tuition, fees, books, and supplies . . . paid directly by the Veteran's Administration, up to a maximum of $500 per school year," plus a monthly subsistence allowance between $50 and $75 (Henry, 1975, p. 57).

ONE

The Study

This is a study of fifty people—thirty men and twenty women—who met the most stringent criterion for academic success: a Ph.D., M.D., or J.D. degree conferred from a highly regarded American university of national stature.[1] However, this is not a study of "successful" individuals in the broader sense; it is about people who chose education as a vehicle for social and economic mobility or personal fulfillment at a particular time when opportunities presented themselves and social conditions were ripe for change. This point is made because other studies have been conducted of "successful" individuals from all kinds of backgrounds (Goertzel, Goertzel, & Goertzel, 1978; Pincus, Elliott, & Schlacter, 1981; Simonton, 1994). However, such studies invariably focus on personality variables that influence broadly defined achievement behavior, and their subjects commonly originate from the middle and upper classes. In the psychological tradition, the origins of achievement behavior have been located in the individual, as distinct from the group. This study explores achievement behavior as a complex phenomenon located at the nexus of the person, the group, and the macro-society; that is, academic achievement as an expression of social self-consciousness.

It is also a study of one small group of people who broke through formidable barriers to high status educations to create part of a new educationally elite class. They are the "advance team" for a new generation of Chicano scholars, born in the fields and the barrios, but educated in the nation's elite universities. Rather than an investigation of extraordinary individuals, this is a study of extraordinary outcomes for individuals from less than ordinary circumstances.

---

1. It was deemed important to be selective (though not elitist) about the institutions attended by the sample subjects in order to avoid concerns about the legitimacy and similarity of the subjects' educational experiences. Institutions are listed in table 1.2.

DESCRIPTION OF THE SUBJECTS

All subjects in this study[2] are Mexican Americans from the first wave of the postwar "baby boom," born during the 1940s and early 1950s. This is the first documented cohort of Mexican Americans to complete doctoral level education and take their places in the professional world (Astin, 1982; Carter & Wilson, 1991). All received their college and graduate educations during the 1960s, and 1970s. The majority of the subjects were the first generation of their family to be born in the United States or they came to this country as young children.[3] However, one-third of the sample had established roots in the United States over multiple generations. All came from families in which neither parent had completed a high school education or held a job higher in status than skilled laborer. The average father of these subjects had a fourth-grade education, and the average mother had completed a little less than five years of school. Most are the sons and daughters of farmworkers and other unskilled laborers (see table 1.1).

Another demographic feature of the sample, the importance of which will become clear in the pages that follow, was the high rate of employment of the mothers in these subjects. Seventy-two percent of the mothers were engaged in income-generating occupations, whereas other data from the same period

---

2. A separate sample of younger women who are more recent graduates will be introduced in chapter 7. However, they met most of the same criteria as were established for this sample of 50, which were:

(1) Male or female of Mexican or Mexican American parentage
(2) Neither parent holding a job higher in occupational status than skilled labor during the time the subject was growing up
(3) Neither parent having completed a high school education
(4) Attended high school during the 1970s, having completed an M.D., J.D., or Ph.D. by the early 1980s
(5) Completed the majority of K-12 schooling in the United States, and
(6) not older than 36 at the time of degree completion.

3. Attempting to establish the generation of Mexican American respondents always presents a challenge that is illustrative of the peculiar nature of the thing we call a "border." In the minds of most North Americans, the border is a reality that separates two countries both physically and psychologically. To be born or to reside on one side of a border or another has meaning in terms of both identity and citizenship status. However, reality is not experienced in the same way by many Mexican Americans and Mexican immigrants. In the case of several of these subjects, at least on parent was born in the United States (and was therefore a U.S. citizen), but raised in Mexico, returning to this country in early adulthood to find work and establish a family. Hence, technically the progeny of such a parent would be considered to belong to the second generation in this country. This technicality, however, obscures the real relationship of the individual and his or her family to their Mexican origins. Hence for the purposes of this study, if one or both parents were raised outside of the United States, the children have been considered first generation in this country.

Table 1.1. *Sample Demographics*

		Generation			Father or Primary Wage Earner's Occupation			Mean Years Education		Mother Employed?		Number of Siblings
	N	Immigrant generation	First generation	Second generation	Unskilled	Semiskilled	Skilled	Father	Mother	Yes	No	Means
TOTAL	50	13 (26%)	22 (44%)	15 (30%)	29 (58%)	11 (22%)	10 (20%)	4.1	5.4	37 (74%)	13 (26%)	5.1
GENDER												
Male	30	6 (20%)	14 (47%)	10 (33%)	14 (33%)	8 (47%)	8 (27%)	3.4 (27%)	5.3	24	6 (80%)	4.8 (20%)
Female	20	7	8 (35%)	5 (40%)	15 (25%)	3 (75%)	2 (15%)	5.2 (10%)	5.6	13	7 (65%)	5.5 (35%)
DEGREE												
J.D.	12	5 (42%)	4 (33%)	3 (25%)	9 (75%)	1 (8%)	2 (17%)	4.6	5.0	5 (75%)	3 (25%)	5.0
M.D.	12	4 (33%)	4 (33%)	4 (33%)	8 (67%)	2 (17%)	2 (17%)	2.8	6.5	9 (75%)	3 (25%)	4.9
Ph.D.	26	4 (15%)	14 (54%)	8 (31%)	12 (46%)	8 (31%)	6 (23%)	4.4	5.0	19 (73%)	7 (27%)	5.2

* Occupations were categorized according to the *Dictionary of Occupational Titles* (1977, 1991)

place the workforce participation rate of married Mexican American women with similar levels of education (mean of 7.8 years in 1960) in the Southwest at only 24 percent (Cooney, 1975). A small portion of the difference between the groups may be attributable to the way in which the data were collected. While the data cited by Cooney are nonspecific about the meaning of "in the labor force," the data presented in table 1.1 reflect all mothers who were generating a portion of the family income. In most cases this included a typical job, out of the home, such as farmworker or cannery worker. However, in two cases the jobs were home-based: doing laundry, ironing, and other domestic chores for pay. The Cooney data also present another interesting finding: when comparing Mexican American and Anglo women *at the same education level*, Anglo women had higher workforce participation in 1960 by a substantial margin of nearly 14 percent (p. 259). Hence, even admitting some differences in definitions, when compared to data for the period, these subjects' mothers appear to have far exceeded the typical labor force participation for both Anglo and Mexican American women of their era.

The following three subjects give a flavor for the occupational and educational backgrounds from which these individuals emerged:

Luisa is a short, sturdy, moderately dark complected woman with a no-nonsense personality and a direct gaze. She exudes an air of certainty in what she says, and her memories of her childhood are clear and precise:

> At the time that we came to the United States [my father] was working at a ranch. My father's previous occupation in Mexico had been farmer, stockman, and that was the logical thing for him to do— to try to get a job as a ranch hand . . . that's what he did until I was nine and he had to leave that job so we could move into town . . . from then on he was essentially a day laborer . . . odd jobs, unskilled labor, anything he could get ahold of . . . he dug holes and cleared debris left by oil crews . . .
>
> [Interviewer: What was your father's highest level of education?]
>
> I think he had six months in all.
>
> [Interviewer: And your mother?]
>
> I think she went for two or three years, but it didn't make any great dent. She learned to read and write, but she's never been terribly good at sums . . . she would take on any and all kinds of jobs, like washing clothes . . . sewing for people . . . [she's] very resourceful.

Luisa attended college in her native Southwest and later completed graduate work at a well-known Eastern university. She became a biology professor and, already into middle age, she had not married, but continued to gain satisfaction from her job teaching and doing research at a major American university.

Adrián, tall, light-skinned, and handsome, fits the image of the corporate attorney that he is. Adrián is sure of himself and of his future. He has served on several boards of directors of major corporations, and perhaps through this experience, has honed his skill at getting directly to the point:

> My father was born in Los Angeles but shortly after he was born the family went back to Sonora, and then he came back with his family when he was ten or so. Both my mother and my father were raised in Brawley . . . that was their home base and they migrated throughout the year. But they always went back to Brawley. . . . They picked prunes for about 25 years at one ranch right above the hills of Stanford. And so they were on their way from there down to the Imperial valley and they stopped the caravan there in Madera, threw out a mattress on the highway, and I was born. After a few days they packed up and came south. . . . My grandmother delivered me, and she delivered everybody else in my family.

> [Interviewer: How far did your mother go in school?]

> About second grade.

> [Interviewer: And your father?]

> About the third.

Adrián, Ivy League educated, professionally successful, and married with two children, had already far exceeded his family's aspirations for him, but he had not yet realized his own ambitions: he confided that he "knew" he was destined for something extraordinary.

Berta is a small, energetic woman with medium coloring and short curly hair. She had first studied to become a chemist and worked in that field for a short time before switching to her real passion: literature. Berta teaches in a major university where she has become an important spokesperson on behalf of Latino students. She is married, with one daughter:

> My father had died, and my mother was pregnant . . . so my mother told my grandmother she could have me and my grandmother said, "Well, if it's a little girl; I don't want to have a little boy." My grandmother didn't like boys. But anyway, she said, "If it's a girl, I'll take her," I guess. So when I was born, my mother raised me for about a year . . . breastfed me . . . then later on, we moved and my mother stayed at her house in San Pedro. . . . [My grandmother] worked in the fields. She always worked in the fields. She worked right alongside my grandfather, whenever and wherever she could.

[Interviewer: And she had no formal education?]

No.

[Interviewer: And your grandfather's education?]

He was totally illiterate. He could only write his name, and that was . . . to get his legal papers, he had to learn to write his name. So he learned to sign his name. He didn't have any education.

During their schooling years the study subjects met most of the criteria which are generally acknowledged to be highly predictive of school failure and dropping out: poverty, low levels of parental education, large families, and limited exposure to English at home. It was deemed important to carefully select individuals from this kind of background for at least two reasons: (1) this is the population that presents the greatest challenge to the education system; and (2) we already know a lot about how middle class groups encourage educational attainment for their children, and the evidence suggests that middle-class Mexican Americans are no different in this regard (Laosa & Henderson, 1991).

LOCATING THE SUBJECTS

Membership lists from professional organizations, two national rosters of Chicano faculty and researchers, and class lists from medical and law schools were consulted initially for leads in identifying potential subjects. While a few subjects were located in this manner, it was a cumbersome process because such lists provide no clue as to the background of the individual and background characteristics were key to the sample selection. (see footnote 2, page 12) The most important source of respondents was through a network sampling procedure. Key individuals were contacted by the researcher at universities and government offices around the country and asked to nominate potential study subjects. These individuals, in turn, called upon others to generate names. Personal nomination had the added advantage of providing an initial screen for background characteristics of the individuals, and frequently provided an introductory phone call which was helpful in securing people's cooperation. Ultimately, hundreds of potential subjects were screened. Of these, fifty-nine were interviewed. (Nine were used in the early piloting phase; fifty were retained for the final study.) Hence, the sample is *not* random, but because the subjects grew up and went to schools all over the United States, and because all persons who were located and met the criteria for inclusion in the study agreed to participate (i.e., there was no systematic reluctance to participate from any portion of the sample), it is reasonable to assume that it is representative of Chicanos who share similar background characteristics. Only half a dozen of the respondents were known to the researcher before the study began.

These subjects were selected because they represent known academic successes, that is, they had already completed their educations, hence there was no question about eventual academic outcomes. Was it critical that they have completed *doctoral*-level educations? Probably not. Many other Chicanos from low-income backgrounds have also used the American higher education system very effectively while only completing bachelor's- or master's-level degrees. However, for the purpose of identifying a sample of individuals who represented the most educationally ambitious of their peers, and about whom there could be little disagreement with respect to the similarity of their experience and the impediments to their achievement, it was deemed prudent to set the educational criterion at an extremely high and explicit level.

The cohort was also restricted to a fairly narrow age range in order to protect against widely differing temporal circumstances; all were pursuing their educations during roughly the same time period and experienced a similar social climate and opportunities with respect to financial aid, recruitment, and competition for college entrance. The mean age of the group is forty-eight years, with the average woman being almost two years older than the average male. Table 1.2 shows the state in which subjects grew up, as well as their graduate institutions and occupations.

There are two compelling reasons for focusing on this cohort of Chicano achievers: the first wave of the "baby boom" generation represents a particular peak in the college-going behavior of Mexican American men and *women*; more recent data show a proportional decline in college enrollment (Carter & Wilson, 1991). Additionally, a heightened emphasis on government support and minority recruitment in higher education, and a cultural "valuing" of ethnic diversity were hallmarks of this period, both factors which are believed to have had a substantial impact on minority college attendance (Astin, 1982). Only once before had college enrollments for minorities seen such a dramatic increase, and this was the result of another major policy decision by the federal government: the GI Bill (Olson, 1974; Henry, 1975). Unfortunately, the GI Bill had its impact almost exclusively on men, and data were not collected on the numbers of people of color who received college degrees as a result of this government-sponsored program.

During the period that these individuals were deciding to go on to college—the 1960s and 1970s—new opportunities were opening up for American minorities and women as a result of a growing concern about equality of educational opportunity (Karabel, 1981). Unlike the GI Bill, which was an attempt to transition young men back into a peacetime economy, this new initiative was based on a belief that the country had failed to exploit much of its intellectual capital by undereducating large segments of the population: women, the lower and working classes, and people of color

Table 1.2. *Educational and Occupational Descriptors*

Subject's Home State	Degree	Graduate Institution	Occupation
MALES			
California	Ph.D. Education	UC Santa Barbara	Professor
New Mexico	Ph.D. Int. Relations	U of Arizona	US State Dept.
California	Ph.D. History	UCLA	Professor
Idaho	Ph.D. Psychology	U of Utah	Psychologist
California	Ph.D. Education	U Southern California	Professor
California	Ph.D. Psychology	UCLA	Psychologist
California	Ph.D. Sociology	UC San Diego	Professor
California	Ph.D. Education	U of Oregon	Professor
Texas	Ph.D. Community Psych	U of Texas, Austin	Psychologist
California	Ph.D. Political Science	UC Riverside	Gov't Consultant
Texas	Ph.D. Psychology	U of Texas, Austin	Professor
California	Ph.D. Comparative ED.	UCLA	Administrator
Texas	Ph.D. Botany	U of Texas, Austin	Professor
California	Ph.D. Political Science	UC Riverside	Professor
Texas	Ph.D. Political Science	Claremont/UCLA	US Foreign Serv.
California	Ph.D. Ed Psychology	UCLA	Researcher
California	J.D.	Stanford	Corporate Lawyer
California	J.D.	Harvard	Com. Organizer
California	J.D.	Harvard	Pub. Interest Lawyer
California	J.D.	Yale	Corp. Management
California	J.D.	Stanford	Corp. Management
California	J.D.	Stanford	Priv. Practice Lawyer
New Mexico	J.D.	Yale	Professor
California	M.D.	UC Davis	Physician
California	M.D.	UCLA	Physician
California	M.D.	Harvard	Physician
Texas	M.D.	U of Texas, Austin	Physician
California	M.D.	U Southern California	Physician
California	M.D.	UC Davis	Psychiatrist
California	M.D.	UC San Francisco	Physician
FEMALES			
California	Ph.D. Social Welfare	Brandeis	Professor
Texas	Ph.D. Linguistics	U of Texas, Austin	Professor
Texas	Ph.D. Spanish	UCLA	Professor
California	Ph.D. Economics	Stanford/UCLA	Researcher
Texas	Ph.D. Counsel Psychology	U of Oregon	Therapist
California	Ph.D. Education	Claremont	Professor
California	Ph.D. Literature	UC San Diego	Professor
California	Ph.D. Anthropology	Stanford	Professor
Texas	Ph.D. Biology	Rutgers	Professor
California	Ph.D. Political Science	UC Riverside	Professor
Texas	J.D.	Georgetown U	Pub. Interest Lawyer
California	J.D.	UCLA	Pub. Interest Lawyer
Texas	J.D.	American U	Gov't. Lawyer
Arizona	J.D.	U of Arizona	Pub. Service Lawyer
California	J.D.	UC Davis	Corporate Lawyer
Texas	M.D.	UCLA	Physician
California	M.D.	UC Davis	Physician
California	M.D.	UC Davis	Physician
California	M.D.	UC Davis	Physician
California	M.D.	UCLA	Physician

(Henry, 1975; Karabel, 1981). Hence, colleges and universities were actively seeking the participation of these groups, and both programs and dollars were devoted to recruitment and support of Mexican Americans and other formerly excluded groups. Given the success that was achieved through these efforts, it is important to examine the impact of such a time and circumstances on the individuals who benefited from them.

Moreover, there is great consistency in the literature on achievement motivation for both majority and minority populations involving samples of subjects studied over the last several decades; the effects of particular family, peer, and schooling variables, for example, have remained relatively stable over time, indicating that similar family and social background factors contribute to educational aspirations across generations. This suggests that the critical mediating variables in minority (Chicano) access and participation in higher education are probably socially constructed phenomena—belief systems, structured opportunities, admissions policies, and so forth. This is a hopeful sign, for these are the variables most amenable to modification by a society wishing to change course or increase equity among its citizens.

SUBGROUP DIFFERENCES

Among the fifty individuals in this study, there are three educational degree groups—roughly, physicians (M.D.'s), lawyers (J.D.'s), and academics (Ph.D.'s)—in addition to both genders. It is reasonable to question whether the subjects' experiences or attitudes might differ according to these characteristics. In other words, might J.D.'s attribute their educational success to something different than Ph.D.'s; or, might the parents of the M.D.'s have differed in some systematic way from the parents of the J.D.'s? While this does not purport to be a quantitative study, these potential differences were tested, using *chi*-square analyses, to discover if gross differences existed in the subjects' responses by degree type and gender. For the most part few differences were found between educational/occupational groups. This is not surprising in light of the small subsample sizes; only large differences can be detected with these reduced numbers. Where differences were found, they are noted in the text. However, there are distinct differences between males and females on some key variables, such as precollege educational patterns and incidence of mentoring. For this reason, special attention is paid to gender differences in chapter 6.

THE WOMEN

There are more men than women in this sample. This was not by design. Locating female subjects was a particular challenge. Most women who were contacted as potential subjects did not meet the background criteria to be included in the study. It became evident in the process of identifying study subjects that it was much more difficult for Chicanas to achieve this level of education without at least one parent breaking into the middle class before them, most typically a mother who had attained the status of a clerical or secretarial position. This led to speculation about the effects that a changing social landscape might have on the educational behavior of Chicanas from low-income and working class homes.

There have been two major sociopolitical trends in the decade and a half since most of the women completed their graduate educations. On the one hand, the women's movement has had an enormous impact on educational and occupational opportunities for women, with substantial gains in college enrollments being posted by women across all ethnic groups (Carter & Wilson, 1993) and an increasing visibility of women even in formerly all-male occupational and educational enclaves (California Postsecondary Eduction Commission, 1993). On the other hand, a new wave of conservatism has washed over the country during the same period, marked by increased challenges to affirmative action as a tool for equalizing educational opportunity, and by declining federal funds available to support the educational aspirations of low-income and minority youth (Orfield & Paul, 1988). For this reason, chapter 7 also reports on a separate study, comparing this cohort of women with a demographically similar group of Chicanas who have recently completed their doctoral educations. Herein we tested the hypothesis that women's career paths might be especially vulnerable to a changing social context. Much about the women's experiences is enduring, as the research on achievement motivation might suggest, but some things have, indeed, changed, including a somewhat different view that the younger women have of themselves.

METHODS

A follow-back, retrospective method, described by Garmezy (1974), was used to gather data through a semistructured interview format. There are, of course, both dangers and limitations in using a retrospective method: memory error, guilt, social norms, and level of interest in the subject matter can all affect the accuracy of respondents' reporting of data (Menneer, 1978). However, there is considerable evidence that the reporting of general attitudes and factual information is relatively stable over time (Gutek, 1978; Haaga, 1986). For example, in a study of Malaysian family life using retrospective survey data, the researchers concluded that "respondent characteristics [e.g., education] more strongly affected the quality of the data than did the length of the recall period . . . even . . . data pertaining to events taking place long before the time of survey, need not exact a major penalty in terms of accuracy [if the respondents are well-educated]" (Haaga, 1986, p. 54).

Moreover, guidelines for assessing the usefulness of retrospective data have been developed which are helpful in determining the appropriateness of the method for particular research. These include: (a) is the subject matter sensitive to time errors (b) will the errors be important to the study (c) can the data be corrected by comparison to other existing data sources and (d) can another, more mechanical method be used (Menneer, 1978). In reviewing these guidelines with respect to the current study, the judgment was made that most subject matter covered in the interviews was not highly dependent upon perception of single events, and hence was less vulnerable to distortion over time. Rather, the questions dealt with ongoing conditions in homes, communities, and schools that could be answered with reference to events over time. Moreover, questions were asked in ways that operationalized concepts, reducing respondents' reliance upon perception alone. For example, to ascertain the level of literacy activity in the home, subjects were asked very specific questions about the presence of particular kinds of print material in the home, the overall frequency with which each parent read, and the nature and overall frequency of family discussions. While some error may surely occur in recall, it is substantially minimized by the specificity of the questions and the personal characteristics of the subjects.

With respect to the importance of data accuracy, certainly the study would be seriously impaired if the data reported were not accurate. While there is no way to ascertain, with absolute certainty, the total accuracy of subjects' statements, there are several factors which lend support to the belief that they were indeed reasonably reliable accounts of subjects' experiences: (1) there was extremely high interest on the part of study participants. Subjects participated with enthusiasm and commonly thanked the researcher for the opportunity to review their lives in such a nonthreatening forum. There was not a single incidence of reluctance to answer any question in the protocol, nor was there a single incidence of reluctance to participate in the study. Level of interest in the study topic has been shown to be a good predictor of data accuracy (Menneer, 1978). (2) Subjects tended to converge in their descriptions of particular phenomena, such as desegregated schooling experiences, central importance of the mother, and so on, in ways that suggest accuracy in reporting. If most people independently report experiencing the same things in similar and often unpredicted ways, logic suggests that there is a reduced likelihood that individuals were failing to recall these experiences accurately. (3) Because the respondents were all well-trained in investigative procedures and were bright, exceptionally articulate individuals, who through many years of graduate training had come to appreciate the importance of academic precision, they represent a sample uniquely predisposed to accuracy in reporting. Moreover, research suggests that more highly educated respondents are, indeed, more accurate in retrospective reporting (Haaga, 1986). (4) Finally, because the researcher shared many of the same background characteristics with the subjects of the study, respondents typically expressed a level of comfort in not having to confront the issue of differing social norms between subject and researcher and were less apt to "reinterpret" information for the interviewer.

Inasmuch as the study dealt very centrally with *what it was like* for the individual subjects to have grown up in their particular circumstances, independent verification of these self-report data is not possible. While corroboration by other family members was considered as a possibility, not even the brothers and sisters of these respondents could know how their siblings internalized their developmental experiences, nor could they have shared the same microenvironments. Nonetheless, given the inherent limitations of the method, the question had to be asked: Is there a better way to collect data on this topic?

The only real methodological alternative to a study such as this one is a prospective study in which subjects are followed from childhood through graduate education. Very few such studies have ever been conducted, for fairly obvious reasons, and none has been conducted on a sample with such a low likelihood of meeting the desired outcome criterion (completion of a doctoral-level degree). Ultimately, the question of whether there was a better way to conduct this study was answered in the negative. Portions of this study can certainly be investigated in greater detail and with greater precision using different methodologies in the future, but in order to establish a roadmap for what really matters in the lives of academically ambitious minority individuals from low-income backgrounds, it was first important to pose those questions directly to the people who had experienced these phenomena.

After a fairly exhaustive review of the literature on achievement, motivation, and minority schooling, a draft interview schedule was developed which included some closed and many open-ended questions about family background, siblings, and childrearing practices; religious experiences; peer relations; attitudes toward, and experiences in, school; mentoring relationships; and personal characteristics and achievement attributions. Questions were designed to test a number of hypotheses about academic achievement motivation which were culled from the literature, but left sufficient flexibility for respondents to add things that were important to them and to suggest their own hypotheses. The interview was piloted on nine subjects, who met most of the same criteria as the sample subjects, and was revised accordingly. The final interview protocol included 141 closed and open-ended questions. (See Appendix) Interviews have been conducted in subjects' homes and places of business, usually by the author, but in a few cases by a research assistant, throughout California, Texas, and the Washington, D.C. area. Interviews ranged in duration from one-and-a-half to more than four hours and were audiotaped and transcribed.

DATA ANALYSIS

Data were first analyzed quantitatively, and by subgroup (male/female; J.D./M.D./Ph.D.), yielding numerous tables that allowed for a cursory description of similarities and differences among groups and highlighted broad areas of commonalities. Where numeric differences were substantial, *chi*-square tests of difference were conducted to determine if "real" differences existed among males and females or between educational degree groups. The most significant differences occurred between males and females, with respect to educational histories (grade-point averages and when they first decided to go to college) and access to mentoring.

Like a picture, this information constituted the broad outlines of the work. Respondents' comments were then grouped and analyzed to fill in the detail around each area of investigation. This gave the picture texture, color, and coherence. Often, the analysis of the respondents' comments—and the tone of their voices—changed entirely the apparent meaning of a particular finding, as in the subjects' interpretations of the roles of parents in shaping their educational ambitions. Without hearing the respondents' voices, it would have been impossible to discern the depth of feeling about mothers' encouragement, or the sympathetic understanding of why fathers often weren't able to be as encouraging of educational aspirations as were the mothers.

Finally, the data were juxtaposed to the existing research to detect patterns of similarities as well as areas of divergence. The process of "making sense" of the data has been a lengthy one in which these data have been continually tested against theories and findings of other researchers and even of the subjects themselves. In a very real sense, this portion of the analysis remains incomplete, as each new reader brings a slightly different lens through which to interpret the findings.

TWO

Home Influences

A substantial literature exists which has demonstrated that family back-ground accounts for a larger portion of the variance in educational outcomes than any other single variable, including the school(s) a student attends (Coleman et al., 1966; Jencks et al., 1972). Given this fact, researchers have devoted a great deal of study to uncover the specific family char-acteristics that make the greatest contributions to students' educational achievement.

There is a consensus that, across racial and ethnic groups, socioeconomic status (usually defined as some combination of educational and occupational status of parents) is the single most powerful contributor to students' educational outcomes (Jencks et al., 1972; Laosa & Henderson, 1991). It is, in fact, because of the highly predictive nature of this variable that the subjects in this study were considered "foreordained" for school failure.

There is less consensus, however, on the question of why socioeconomic status has such powerful effects. Some have suggested that the social repro-duction of status differences between population groups is the direct result, and express intent, of capitalist economic policy to maintain social class ad-vantages (Bowles & Gintis, 1976). That is, the schooling system in the United States is ordered in such a way as to channel upper-income students into educational opportunities (e.g., college preparatory coursework) that will prepare them for higher-status occupations, and lower-income students into the vocational preparation tracks that preclude them from competing for jobs with their upper income peers. Moreover, this "meritocratic" system, in which students are sorted according to supposed intellectual ability, operates to convince lower-income students that they "deserve" lower status jobs because of their own failure to perform adequately on tests devised to highlight the skills and attributes of the middle class.

Others have suggested that the effects of family socioeconomic status on educational outcomes are more the inadvertent result of a culture of poverty

25

(Lewis, 1961; Glazer & Moynihan, 1963) versus a culture of plenty. In poverty cultures, maladaptive responses to schooling are transmitted through the generations by parents who were themselves ill-suited to school, did poorly, and failed to learn the skills necessary to propel themselves or their progeny through the educational system. Conversely, the sons and daughters of the middle class are raised to believe that schools are supposed to serve their needs. This sense of entitlement serves them well in shaping the institution of school into their own image.

Further explanations for the powerful correlation between the socio-economic status of the family of origin and achievement behaviors of children include notions of social and cultural capital (Coleman, 1987; Lareau, 1987, 1989). According to these models, middle- and upper-class parents who have been successful in school understand the "hidden curriculum" of schooling and know how to coach their children in appropriate responses to the system. They also have extensive community resources and networks that extend their children's educational reach beyond the confines of the school and allow these parents to exploit "the system" to the educational advantage of their offspring. What all of these disparate theories hold in common is a mechanism, however conceived, for passing the advantage of one generation to the next, and ensuring that, with only rare exceptions, no interlopers will usurp the advantage of the elite classes.

PARENT-CHILD INTERACTIONS AND TEACHING STRATEGIES

Parents also have the most direct impact on the formation of their children's educational aspirations. Numerous studies have demonstrated the relationships between middle-class communication patterns and social behaviors learned at home, and the particular demands of classroom interaction. The results of these studies suggest that the behaviors required for success in school are the same kinds of behaviors that are typically transmitted by parents in white, middle-class homes, and that students who are not exposed to this acculturating home experience may be at risk for school failure (Erickson, 1987).

Laosa (1978) has shown that Mexican American mothers do, indeed, employ different behaviors than non-Hispanic white mothers when teaching specific tasks to their children, and that these behaviors are sometimes in conflict with the demands of school situations. Whereas the white, middle-class mothers used an inquiry approach to teaching tasks, an approach which encouraged children's independent action, Mexican American mothers tended to provide the solutions for their children, thereby impeding them from taking responsibility for their own learning. The middle-class approach is more aligned with the requirements for independent (as opposed to group) problem solving that are characteristic of American classrooms. However, Laosa also found that when socioeconomic class was controlled, there was little difference between the teaching behaviors of non-Hispanic white and Mexican American mothers. Middle-class Chicana mothers, with higher levels of education, also used questioning behaviors more extensively than modeling when teaching their children.

PSYCHOSOCIAL FACTORS IN ACHIEVEMENT MOTIVATION

More generally, the ways in which families help children to acquire the motivation to achieve have been studied extensively by a number of psychologists. Eminent among these are McClelland, Atkinson, and their colleagues (McClelland et al., 1953; McClelland, 1965; Atkinson & Feather, 1966), who proposed that motivation for achievement could be engendered in children through early training by setting high standards and providing sufficient independence for the child to develop a sense of task mastery. Anderson and Evans (1976), in a study employing Mexican American pupils, were also able to demonstrate a positive association between independence training and academic achievement. However, the unique nature of interdependence of family members in the Mexican American family described by Grebler, Moore, and Guzmán (1970), calls into question whether independence has the same meaning for Chicanos as it may for other cultural groups. For example, while independence of the family *unit* might be valued within Chicano culture, family members are commonly rewarded for pursuing familial rather than personal goals.

Others, notably Wolf (1963) and Davé (1964), further developed this line of research in an investigation of the "achievement press" of the home. They contended that certain parental behaviors could combine to create a press for achievement that would result in higher academic performance. In fact, with non-Hispanic white school-age subjects, Davé and Wolf were able to obtain a .80 correlation between their cluster of home environmental process variables which included such things as intellectuality of the home (e.g., availability of books and other educational materials), standards for work habits, and opportunities for language development and academic achievement. Although Marjoribanks (1972) was able to demonstrate the independence of these variables from socioeconomic status for non-Hispanic white students, Henderson (1966) was unable to establish this same independence for Mexican Americans, suggesting that, at least for Chicanos, academic and intellectual opportunities in the home are a function of the family's economic resources.

NON-INSTRUCTIONAL INFLUENCES

In a review of the literature on noninstructional influences on student achievement, Steinberg, Brown, Cider, Kaczmarek, and Lazzaro (1988) concluded that "studies of family processes indicate that students perform better when they are raised in homes characterized by supportive and demanding parents who are involved in schooling and who encourage and expect academic achievement" (p. ii). The studies they reviewed, however, involved mostly white, middle-class families. In an effort to remedy this shortcoming in the research, Steinberg, Dornbusch, and Brown (1992) conducted their own study of ethnic differences in adolescent achievement. Borrowing from earlier research by Baumrind (1989) which demonstrated that an "authoritative"—warm, strict, and democratic—parenting style was associated with higher academic achievement in children more than either authoritarian or permissive styles, Steinberg, Dornbusch, and Brown tested this finding for Asian American, African American, and Hispanic American students. They found Hispanic parents to be more authoritarian than white parents, presumably resulting in a lesser achievement orientation. They did caution, however, that parenting styles did not operate independently of peer influences in predicting academic achievement, particularly for minority adolescents.

Clark (1983), in his study of family life and school achievement among African American students growing up in an urban ghetto, also investigated parenting styles and their relationship to academic success and failure. While noting that Baumrind's authoritative parenting style was most evident in the homes of successful black students, he also emphasized the importance of parental *control.* Clark asserts that one of the primary characteristics of the homes of successful black students is an environment in which "parents establish clear, specific role boundaries and status structures with parents as dominant authority" (p. 202). He further elaborates the point a few pages later:

> The degree of parental influence over the student's *time and space* is important for school success. As parents are able to channel the student into parentally sponsored, academically oriented spheres of activity, the student acquires a sense of self-reliance, home approval, and initiative. If parents are unable to channel the student's use of time and space, negative forces (e.g., gangs) have a greater opportunity to recruit the student. (p.207)

Hence, the line between the *authoritative* parent (warm, strict, and democratic) and the *authoritarian* one (who may be warm and strict, but undemocratic) may sometimes be obscured when an unforgiving environment like an urban ghetto or barrio raises the stakes on loss of parental control.

Parental involvement in children's schooling has also been shown to be positively correlated with higher student achievement. Stevenson and Baker (1987), using a nationally representative sample of elementary and secondary students, demonstrated that attendance at parent-teacher conferences, participation in parent-teacher organizations, and influence over their children's selection of courses were predictive of academic achievement. Similarly, Lareau (1987), in a study of the schooling experiences of working class and middle calss students and their families, has shown that family "cultural capital", as manifested in parental contact with schools and knowledge of how to "work the system" are associated both with children's academic achievement and family socioeconomic status. Middle class parents are much more likely to visit the schools and extract resources on behalf of their children than are lower-income parents. Consistent with these findings, Mexican American parents are frequently characterized as having low rates of participation in school activities (Delgado-Gaitan, 1991).

Researchers familiar with Mexican American culture have attributed this low level of participation on the part of Chicano parents as being due to a lack of familiarity with the American school system, a fear of not being able to communicate with school personnel, competing family and work demands on their time, and limited resources to pay for babysitters and bus fares. Many educators, however, have interpreted the parents' absence as evidence of a lack of value for education (Carter, 1970). This then becomes a convenient excuse for the poor performance of Chicano students—their parents don't care about school or support its aims.

Delgado-Gaitan (1991), however, reports on a study in which Mexican American parents were empowered to effect changes in their children's schools that resulted in increased academic achievement for their children. In this study in a semi-rural, California central valley town, all parent meetings and school business were conducted bilingually, and roles of authority in the parent organization were distributed equally to Spanish and English speakers. Parents were armed with information about both their rights and their responsibilities within the school system, and they were educated on the leverage points within the bureaucratic system of the schools, that is, where to go if they wanted to get something done. Parents in this community used this information and access to the system to organize themselves into a powerful lobbying force on behalf of their children, belying the myth that they didn't care about education. Yet, in order for this level of parent participation to be realized, the school had to demonstrate a strong commitment to surmount language barriers and provide real access to both power and information for the Chicano parents.

In sum, there is a large body of literature pointing to several ways in which parents and families affect educational outcomes for their children: opportunities for independence and task mastery, high aspirations and standards, encouragement for schooling, creation of an intellectually stimulating environment, and involvement in schooling. Nonetheless, the research is occasionally contradictory, but most often silent, on the issue of how ethnic minority parents, and Chicano parents in particular, can and do impact their children's schooling.

We now turn to the study sample. Given that the parents of the study subjects had relatively little experience with schooling themselves, and lacked many of the social and economic resources that middle class parents call upon in orienting their children toward high educational aspirations, the questions to be answered were: Did these parents exhibit the same kinds of behaviors noted in the literature on high achieving students? If so, how, given their limited circumstances, would the parents evidence these behaviors?

THE NEXUS OF INDEPENDENCE, TASK MASTERY, AND HARD WORK

It would be impossible to know what kinds of maternal teaching strategies were used with these subjects, solely on the basis of retrospective interview. This question is unanswerable with the current data. However, at a more global level, about two-thirds of the subjects reported that their parents stressed the development of independence as they were growing up. This meant "doing things on your own, not asking for help, especially outside of the family." Oftentimes this took the form of accepting large amounts of responsibility within the home as in the case of the civil rights lawyer who recounted the responsibilities thrust on her in late childhood:

> I learned all the responsibilities of the home. When I was 12 years old, I fixed a baptismal dinner for my little brother. And babysat five kids while I was making dinner and he was getting baptized at church. So, by age 12, I had all the housekeeping skills. I could cook dinner, I could clean, I could take care of children, I could wash. . . . My mother never even thanked me for anything I did. She just took it as a matter of course. . . .

Or, as a male education professor recalled,

> [M]y father . . . was a butcher, and they taught me the business of the family, at a very young age, and I began practicing some of those things at the age of seven. . . . I was running the business at eight years old.

For these individuals independence and hard work were closely related concepts:

> I think they stressed independence, but they did it like . . . you have to be self-reliant if you want to make it, there's no one to fall back on . . . if you don't work there's not going to be food on the table. Despite it all I got some good values from my parents. Hard work, and independence, I got those from them.

Especially for the farmworker parents, independence was not an abstract concept but a reality of everyday life. Being independent meant being able to fend for oneself in the world of work. As one subject very succinctly put it, "when you're working in the fields, whether you're picking string beans or fruit, or whatever, everyone carries his own load."

Lessons in the value of hard work and independence were sometimes also articulated verbally. Some parents were very explicit about what they expected their children to take from their work experiences:

> [T]hey encouraged us to be good workers . . . an attitude that some-how we needed to be efficient, have something, have some skill that people would be willing to pay for, so in that sense we were encouraged in independence. We had to work in the fields every-day, even in elementary school.

This training in responsibility and independent behavior was a natural outgrowth of the parents' own dedication to the work ethic. Virtually every subject in the study commented upon their parents' extraordinary capacity for hard work. It should be mentioned, also, that no question in the interview specifically asked about this. However, when describing their parents, subjects invariably noted that they were the hardest working people they had ever known:

> My mother was a very hardworking woman, she still works hard . . . she worked all the time. She was a clerk, she still is a clerk . . . sells shoes . . . Monday through Saturday . . . and then on Sunday, she used to go clean up offices, every Sunday, I remember that because I used to help her sometimes. She worked all the time, all the time.

Another subject reflected back on his life and experiences and offered the following description of his father, a man in whom he found little else to admire:

> He doesn't stop. Physically he keeps himself busy until he practically goes to sleep. Even if there is nothing to do, he finds something to do. He will knock down a tree and put it up again.

The role of hard work, both as a model for behavior which would later translate into persistence in schoolwork, as well as a means for instilling a sense of independence and taking care of oneself, cannot be overstated. Whereas more middle-class parents might structure learning opportunities for their children which would emphasize independent behavior, these parents encouraged independent behavior in a more direct manner:

> Self reliance was a sort of a learned kind of thing, because, like I said before, when my mother left Wilmington, she took her kids [eight

children] and she didn't ask for help from anybody. And that was a very vivid lesson to all of us, that is, if you wanted something, you went out and you paid the price for it.

One subject, a corporate lawyer, explained how the hard work ethic of his mother translated into a sense of high standards in whatever one did:

> My mother . . . would have made All-American in any sport, because if we were picking tomatoes she was the champion of both men and women. If we were picking cotton she was the champion. Whatever, she was the outstanding. And it has to do with her athletic ability, but also with her tremendous sense of wanting to achieve and to win, and I think I learned that from her . . . and if I came home and said I pitched a one-hitter, she said, "Why didn't you pitch a no-hitter?" And if I said I got 4 As and a B, she wanted to know why I didn't get all As . . . she just expected us to be at the top, by her example.

In a very few cases, this sense of independence was learned because the parents failed to provide positive role models and the children were forced, of necessity, to take on the home responsibilities themselves. A lawyer, whose father was an alcoholic and periodically abandoned the home, recalled how her parents, somewhat inadvertently, instilled independence in her:

> I think it was their irresponsible attitude toward life. I had to fend for myself and learn to fend for my family. I knew at an early age, I think all of us knew, no matter what happened it wasn't the end of the world. There was always tomorrow. We'd always get by. It happened so much. Like my father would leave us, and we'd manage. I guess it gave us sort of a fighting attitude. We became very competitive in school and we had a very strong survival instinct.

FAMILY STRUCTURE AND SIBLING ACHIEVEMENT

It is nearly axiomatic that two-parent families produce higher academic achievement in children than do single-parent families. Virtually all large-scale studies reach this same conclusion. The commonsense explanation for this finding is that two-parent families generally have more resources, both human and financial, than single-parent families, especially when the single parent is a woman (Mulkey, 1992). Yet carefully crafted, smaller studies that control for socioeconomic status and focus on family processes have not always reached this same conclusion (Clark, 1983; Hetherington, 1981). Nonetheless, single parenting places heavy burdens on the lone parent that are not always shouldered adequately. Given the enormous social and economic disadvantages that the study subjects experienced in realizing their academic ambitions, one would be inclined to presume that they must have, at least, been raised in intact families. Not so.

Twenty-six percent of the subjects, slightly more than a quarter, were raised in homes that had been disrupted by divorce, separation, or death or abandonment by one or both parents. Six of the subjects were raised in fatherless homes for all or the majority of their childhoods; the remaining seven who had grown up in nonintact homes either lived with relatives or had a stepfather come into the family. Thus, while the incidence of family disruption was not extraordinary for the time or their social conditions, neither were these subjects disproportionately protected from the turmoil and risks associated with family breakdown. Yet, as Clark (1983) takes pains to reiterate, "support and control . . . are not a function of single parenthood or family intactness; they are cultural, not structural phenomena" (p. 198).

Another consistent finding in the research literature is that academic achievement is correlated with family size: the larger the number of siblings, the lower the overall achievement of the children (Steelman, 1985; Zajonc, 1976). The confluence model postulated by Zajonc further asserts that subsequently born children will perform more poorly academically than their earlier born siblings, with the exception of those born last. Zajonc's rationale for his model is that family resources are at the heart of the inequities between siblings. Each family has only a limited amount of intellectual capital to share with its children. Therefore, firstborn children and children in smaller families (no more than two or three siblings) will receive a greater portion of parental stimulation and other resources than children born later and into larger families. This is a relatively straightforward economic argument, and while hotly debated, a number of other researchers have come to similar conclusions. Whether or not the confluence model holds up to careful scrutiny, it has continued to influence research in the field of cognitive psychology (Steelman, 1985).

Marjoribanks (1988, 1990), however, has investigated the mediating effects of specific family characteristics, such as parental press for education and the intellectual environment of the home, on sibling achievement differences and concluded that any model is incomplete without taking these into account. Some researchers, moreover, have questioned the confluence model's ability to account for performance variations in ethnic minority siblings (Steelman, 1985; Valencia, Henderson, & Rankin, 1981). In a stunning reversal of the bulk of research on sibsize effects, Caplan, Choy, and Whitmore (1992) published a recent study in *Scientific American* which suggested that there may be vast cultural differences in the sibsize/academic-achievement relationship. In their careful study of Southeast Asian boatpeople living in the United States, they found a positive relationship between the numbers of siblings in a family and the children's academic achievement. That is, as the family size increased, so did the grade-point averages of the children. The researchers attributed this finding to the observation that within the Southeast Asian families, more siblings resulted in more, rather than fewer, educational resources. Because older siblings took on the role of teacher for younger siblings, and because homework was viewed as a family activity, the children in large families had greater support for their academic endeavors and a larger total number of teachers.

The subjects in the current study came from large families; the average number of siblings per family was a little over five, and the typical family consisted of seven persons. Data from the 1960 census for Mexican Americans living in the Southwest put the average family size at 4.8 (Mittlebach & Marshall, 1966). Although census data include in their figures households without children, thereby reducing the average, by any standard, the family size of these subjects would be considered large. Almost exactly one-third (34 percent) of the subjects was firstborn. The largest portion (58 percent) of the subjects was born somewhere in the middle position, with only 8 percent of subjects being lastborn in the family. Hence, the characteristics of this sample consistently contradict earlier research on family structure and school achievement.

What were the patterns of achievement for the siblings of these high achievers? There was no discernible pattern that characterized the sample as a whole. The sample broke down into almost exact thirds: one-third of subjects came from families in which all or all but one other sibling had completed or was clearly on track to complete a college degree; one-third came from families in which some other siblings had received or were on-track to receive a college degree; and one-third of subjects came from families in which only one other sibling, or they alone, were the only family members to complete a college degree. Among the lastborn achievers, a common explanation for the failure of preceding children to attain a college degree was poverty and lack of opportunity which had fallen more heavily on the earlier born siblings. A young physician, the last of ten children, was illustrative of this situation. The only other sibling who was successful in completing a college education was a sister who obtained her B.A. while a nun in the Catholic church. Speaking of her siblings, the physician commented:

> They're all very bright. Only when they were growing up, financially
> it wouldn't have been feasible for them after high school to go to
> college. They had to work. . . . I was the last one. If I had been one
> of the first ones, I would never have gone to college.

A number of the subjects reported that older brothers or sisters played the significant role of transmitting expectations and paving the way to college. One subject, a law school graduate and corporate executive, talked about the way his older sister, frustrated in her own ambitions, had been instrumental in developing his:

> My oldest sister . . . was, I think all along, much sharper and intelligent and academically oriented than I was. . . . I think I was very much molded by her influence. . . . [S]he never completed college. I think she could have had a tremendous academic career, but as she was the oldest, she bore most of the brunt of my father's pressure and didn't accomplish as much as I did. . . . [S]he helped me a lot. One of the important decisions . . . about which high school to go to, had to do with her. She was the one who encouraged me to take the . . . alternative. She gave me the reasons why and she recognized at that point that it was important academically for me to do it.

Another subject, a political scientist, recounted how the fact that his older sister had attended Berkeley made it seem possible for the rest of the children of the family, especially for him, to realize his educational goals:

> My sister was a tremendous influence on me. . . . I can remember, how many times I used to tell people my sister was at Berkeley. That was sort of a success image, a very important success image aspect of the relationship.

Without a doubt, the experience of these individuals calls into question nearly all of the research on family size and sibling effects. For these subjects, large family size was not a particular impediment, and older siblings often played an important role in encouraging and fostering their ambitions. Interestingly, the thwarted ambitions of an older sibling were as likely to provide the impetus for a college education as was the model of achievement provided by a highly motivated brother or sister. Neither were these subjects disproportionately firstborns or lastborns, as the literature would suggest they should have been, and many came from homes disrupted by death, divorce, or abandonment. This one sample of high achievers could not, in itself, dismantle countervailing theory; however, when coupled with research like that of Caplan, Choy, and Whitmore (1992), one is forced to question whether existing research on family structure has adequately accounted for family dynamics and values across cultures, or if our understanding of these phenomena has been too narrowly focused through a middle-class, Anglo American lens.

PARENTAL SUPPORT AND ENCOURAGEMENT

The literature on academic achievement motivation is replete with references to support in the home for academic or intellectual pursuits. Such support may take the form of encouragement for performing well in school, helping with homework and school assignments, providing stimulating learning experiences in the home for children, and helping them to set educational goals. To what extent were these parents, overworked and undereducated themselves, able to provide these kinds of supports for their own children?

Mother/Father Differences

Subjects were very emphatic on the topic of parental support and encouragement. Most subjects reported that both parents were supportive of educational goals, though mothers were substantially more so (see table 2.1).

While fathers frequently indicated that they wanted their children to do well in school, they were more ambivalent in the messages that they conveyed to their children. One ex-farmworker commented:

> [M]y father politically and philosophically supports education, but he wanted me to work more . . . it was difficult for him, he needed me to help pay the bills.

A young lawyer whose father was a railroad worker described the lukewarm encouragement she received from him in the following way:

> My dad was very antieducation, especially for women. "You're going to get married, so I don't see why you need an education" . . . but he never pressured us to quit school . . . my dad let everybody finish school. So that was kind of a big accomplishment.

In the cases where the father was not fully supportive of the children's educational ambitions, usually the mother would intervene on their behalf. A biologist described the dynamics in her family:

> Once it became clear that I was doing well in school, you know, my father just felt eighth grade education was . . . a lot of education. He had none, so eighth grade was already an educated person and he wanted me to get out and work, just thinking of money. [But] my mother said, "Look, she's doing all right, why don't we just let her go on to high school?" . . . It was usually her influence and her intervention that allowed them to come up with a little extra money to buy clothes or buy books . . . and it was her perseverance when it came time to go to college . . . my father wouldn't sign my National Defense Loan . . . because he was afraid of the consequences if I weren't able to make it through college, default on the loan. [But] my mother . . . was always saying, "Oh we'll make it, she'll make it".

Another subject described how his mother provided the support for schooling that his father lacked:

Table 2.1. *Parental Support for Education*

	Mother			
	Not Very Important	Moderately Important	Very Important	Total *N*
TOTAL	4 (8%)	3 (6%)	43 (86%)	50 (100%)
GENDER				
Male	1 (3%)	1 (3%)	28 (94%)	30 (100%)
Female	3 (15%)	2 (10%)	15 (75%)	20 (100%)
DEGREE				
J.D.	2 (17%)	0 (0%)	10 (83%)	12 (100%)
M.D.	1 (8%)	0 (0%)	10 (92%)	11 (100%)
Ph.D.	1 (4%)	3 (11%)	23 (85%)	27 (100%)

	Father			
	Not Very Important	Moderately Important	Very Important	Total *N*
TOTAL	12 (26%)	8 (17%)	26 (57%)	46 (100%)
GENDER				
Male	5 (19%)	5 (19%)	17 (63%)	27 (100%)
Female	7 (37%)	3 (16%)	9 (47%)	19 (100%)
DEGREE				
J.D.	4 (33%)	1 (8%)	7 (58%)	12 (100%)
M.D.	3 (30%)	2 (20%)	5 (50%)	10 (100%)
Ph.D.	5 (21%)	5 (21%)	14 (58%)	24 (100%)

I think it was more of a covert thing, although it was well understood. My dad was more lax, and I'm sure if we had wanted to drop out of school in third grade, and he were the only one around, we would have done it. But, you know, having her there, it was understood that was not to be talked about.

It is evident from the numbers (tables 2.1 and 2.2) that mothers were most often the guiding force in the home behind the children's powerful educational ambitions. However, the numbers do not reflect the *depth* of feeling that subjects expressed about their mother's encouragement. There was little hesitation on the part of subjects in answering the question "Which of your parents had the greatest influence on setting your educational goals?" Usually the response was swift and emphatic: "My mother." One subject explained what he saw as the apparent contradiction in the common stereotype of passive, submissive Mexican mothers, and the role they consistently played in their children's goal-setting:

My mother always predominated in my family. That's something that's sort of subtle, that's not brought out within our culture. I think in a lot of the Chicano families, the mother is really the head. The father is more a figurehead and he ultimately puts down the blows. But the mother is really the one that controls the father. It's sort of manipulative.

Many subjects commented similarly that the father was the acknowledged head of the household, or "figurehead," but that the mother was the one who exerted the greatest influence over their lives, even in everyday decisions. A female physician reflected in a similar manner on the way power was exercised within her "traditional" family. In response to the question "Which of your parents was the dominant one in your family?" she replied:

My mother. Because my parents were very traditional Mexican people. She always made him feel like he was making the decisions, but all the time she was making them. She was a master at that.

It would appear that these subjects' analysis was probably reasonably accurate and representative of many of the homes from which the subjects came. On the whole, support and encouragement came either from mother alone, or both parents together, but seldom from father alone. Interestingly, mothers may have been able to overcome the resistance or lack of enthusiasm of fathers in fueling their children's educational ambitions, but fathers, it appears, did not exercise the same power in the face of maternal resistance or ambivalence (see table 2.2).

To some extent the data on fathers are artifactual. As noted earlier, fully one quarter of the sample either grew up without a father in the home for long periods of their childhood, or the natural father had been replaced by a stepfather or other male relative who assumed (no doubt to varying degrees) the father's role. Hence, the *opportunity* for father encouragement and support was not always present.

It is also important to note, however, the way in which subjects described their fathers' attitudes toward schooling. There was a matter-of-factness in the tone of most subjects' responses; seldom was any blame assigned to fathers for their failure to be more encouraging of educational ambitions. Rather, subjects evidenced a sense of resigned understanding; that this wasn't really part of the father's role. Mothers counsel, encourage, and inspire; fathers go off to work and ensure that the family survives. In fact, the father's duty could be construed as imparting a sense of realistic, attainable goals: a steady job or domestic skills that would allow the subjects to support and nurture their own families. Further evidence of this construction of the father's role lies in the fact that many of the fathers who did not articulate lofty educational goals for their children nonetheless supported their schooling and went to great lengths to help with homework or special assignments.

Table 2.2. *Most Influential Parent in Setting Educational Goals*

	Mother	Father	Both	Neither	Total
TOTAL	28 (56%)	8 (16%)	9 (18%)	5 (10%)	50 (100%)
GENDER					
Males	18 (60%)	5 (17%)	5 (17%)	2 (7%)	30 (100%)
Females	10 (50%)	3 (15%)	4 (20%)	3 (15%)	20 (100%)
DEGREE					
J.D	7 (58%)	0 (0%)	3 (25%)	2 (17%)	12 (100%)
M.D.	9 (75%)	1 (8%)	0 (0%)	2 (17%)	12 (100%)
Ph.D.	12 (46%)	7 (27%)	6 (23%)	1 (4%)	26 (100%)

Kinds of Familial Support

Because parents had few resources and relatively little experience with schooling themselves, most of what they could offer their children was verbal support and encouragement for their educational undertakings. Most subjects felt this support very strongly at home. Sometimes parents articulated this support; the father of an Ivy League lawyer was quoted as saying:

> "Well, don't be what I am. Don't have to earn your living by having to dig ditches and filling them up. Use your brains and use your head. Do something better. Don't be a dummy like me. Finish school and you go out and learn yourself something."

Other times the support was less directive but nonetheless fully understood by the children. One physician talked about how her mother encouraged her without really setting any specific goals:

> She expected us to do our best and other than that she never directed us, but she always encouraged us. . . . She really goes out of her way to not bring in her own feelings, to make us feel that we are making a decision on our own. "Don't do anything for me," she says. "Do it for yourself." She always supported my decisions, but she never directed them.

Apart from just verbal encouragement, many subjects recalled instances of their parents actually helping with schoolwork, to the extent that they could, which was usually very limited. A law professor recalled his first homework lesson in the third grade:

> I had to read something and I don't remember it all, but it had something to do with reading a story that had something to do with flax. I remember not really knowing what to do and I asked my father. It was late—I had waited to do it 'til really, really late and my father stayed up with me and tried to figure out what I was supposed to do.

To make his point about his father's willingness to help his children, even though his own skills were limited, he went on:

> [O]ne time that was characteristic of the way he would help . . . my sister was trying to do some homework and she was trying to find the definition of *fortnight* and dad didn't know exactly what it was and couldn't find it in the small dictionary that we had . . . we didn't have a telephone in those days, but he went and knocked on doors of people that he thought would have dictionaries to get them up so they could find a definition of *fortnight* for him.

A physician whose father died when she was nine recalled his attempts to help her with her homework, and her mother's efforts as well:

> I remember my father going over my arithmetic with me all the time. They really didn't have that much in the way of resources at all, the experience that was needed, but they were always there. They were interested in my homework. They helped us. They made us study. I remember them buying us books. And I remember my mother taking us to the library, which nobody else's mother did. I remember going to the library every Saturday when we moved to Barstow . . . and her . . . knowing the librarian, because we went there every Saturday to pick out new books.

Another subject's mother, unable to help her budding scientist son in any direct way, provided encouragement for his curiosity:

> When I was in high school, I used to bring a dead cat and dissect it at the [dining room] table. . . . She thought it was fantastic that I knew all the muscles.

The law professor whose father combed the neighborhood looking for a dictionary that had the word *fortnight* recalled the poignant moment when his father, a laborer who had gone to the eighth grade, felt he could no longer help his son:

> [W]hen I graduated from the eighth grade . . . he took me aside and he said, "Look, you know, from now on you have more education than I do and you know better than I about what you want and what you are supposed to do. I have been able to help you up till now but I can't help you anymore." So, he was sort of saying he trusted my judgment.

CREATING THE ENVIRONMENT FOR ACHIEVEMENT

Promoting Literacy in the Home

Because of the consensus in the research literature as to the importance of providing a rich intellectual environment and opportunities to develop literacy for future academic achievement, subjects were asked about the availability of reading material in their homes. They were asked if they had in their homes (1) an encyclopedia, (2) a dictionary, (3) a daily newspaper, (4) magazine subscriptions, and (5) more than twenty-five books. It was assumed that most would not have had such things in their homes because parental education was very low and both time and financial resources were extremely limited. Astonishingly, 98 percent of the subjects had *at least* two of the five things, and almost 70 percent had an encyclopedia in the home as they were growing up. Moreover, half of the subjects reported that at least one parent was an avid reader, a fact that is more than a little surprising in light of the low level of formal education of the parents.

Most of these parents read in Spanish and shared this activity with their children. It was therefore not surprising to find that many of the subjects, and almost all of the women, were avid readers throughout school, and even credited reading with being key to their academic success. Reading, however, is not the only form of literacy training, nor was it the only way in which these parents encouraged their children's love of learning. Vygotsky, the famed Russian psychologist who has revolutionized modern thinking about literacy, contended that written language develops as speech does, in the context of its use, hence the importance for learners to be immersed in language in order for literacy to be easy (Goodman & Goodman, 1990). This is precisely what almost two thirds of the parents of these subjects did. Sixty-two percent of the subjects recounted how discussions of politics, labor organizing, and world events were routine topics in their households. Several of the parents held strong views on social issues, or were well versed in history or literature and shared this love of inquiry and ideas with their progeny. There were no differences between the sexes on this factor; however, table 2.3 displays differences by educational degree category. While the sample is small, it is nonetheless interesting that the J.D.'s were most likely to have engaged in this kind of intellectual activity in their homes.

The picture that emerges of the home environments of most of these subjects is one in which a high premium was placed on ideas and information, in spite of the very limited formal education of the parents. It is also interesting to note that, while mothers were commonly described as being avid readers, and on the average had slightly more education than their husbands, it was almost always fathers who were noted to have inspired the children's learning through their teaching. It was most often the fathers who seemed to have the particular penchant for studying and discussing a specific topic: the opera, music, history, or science. Hence, while mothers encouraged and inspired their children, fathers showed them the wonders of the world and invited them to pursue its mysteries.

Table 2.3. *Literacy in the Home*

	One or Both Parents Readers	Politics/Current Events Discussion Common	Encyclopedia in Home	Total
TOTAL	25 (50%)	30 (60%)	34 (68%)	50 (100%)
GENDER				
Male	12 (40%)	18 (60%)	23 (77%)	30 (100%)
Female	13 (65%)	12 (60%)	11 (55%)	20 (100%)
DEGREE				
J.D.	7 (58%)	10 (82%)	9 (75%)	12 (100%)
M.D.	7 (58%)	4 (36%)	7 (58%)	12 (100%)
Ph.D.	11 (42%)	16 (62%)	17 (65%)	26 (100%)

One subject, a political science professor whose father had never attended school and whose mother had less than one year of education, recalled her home environment in the following way:

> My father is a self-educated man. He was very, very intelligent and really well read, but he did it himself. And my mother too. My mother enjoyed reading . . . she had read a lot of what we consider classics in Spanish whenever she could get ahold of them and she was an avid reader. . . . My father . . . loved music . . . he knew all the artists and the names of all the operas, the music of all the operas. I remember the old cartoons, they always had classical music in the background. My father would take us to see those nasty cartoons just to listen to that classical music. . . . I always thought it was such a terrible combination of those ugly cartoon figures and this beautiful music. My father's dream was always to go to the San Francisco Opera, the opening of the opera in San Francisco. He did get to go to Los Angeles once, but he never got to go to San Francisco. We were going to take him one day, but then he had cancer and he couldn't walk very well.

Similarly, a linguistics professor whose parents both dropped out of school before the sixth grade commented on the early education she received in her home, particularly from her father who became a lay preacher and Sunday school teacher:

> My father was an exceptional man. Education was very important to him . . . he would give us like statement problems, "What if I bought this . . . ." We'd sit there and try to figure it out . . . then when we started going to church everything was in Spanish, and everybody was supposed to read chapters and report. So I had a great deal of instruction in the Spanish language without knowing it. Also it sort of

set the stage for literature. By the time I went into literature, that kind of stuff was not difficult at all. I would simply write in a Biblical style.

A professor of social work whose father worked as a surveyor (having taught himself the trade in night school) recalled how he stimulated her interest in reading and learning:

> [M]y father, he was very political and he was very knowledgeable about what was going on in the world. I was brought up reading the newspaper everyday and he read at least two or three other newspapers, he was always up on the news. . . . The other thing my father is very interested in is science and every Sunday he would take me down to the park and we would go to the zoo and learn a lot about the animals and . . . the biology of plants and animals. He taught me a lot about the leaves and what they are called. He used to take me to the seashore and teach me about the sea shells and sea life.

To the extent that attitudes and dispositions in favor of literacy activities are aspects of cultural capital, these homes shared much of the cultural wealth of the middle and upper classes, albeit acquired through nonformal education.

Foregoing Children's Economic Contributions

Some parents, however, were not able to provide this kind of intellectual stimulation for their children, and even rudimentary homework lessons were beyond their level of academic skill. The children knew that their parents wouldn't be able to help them. But one way that even these parents were able to show their support for their children's education was in protecting their time for study and foregoing badly needed financial help:

> My parents pressured me to stay in school and they didn't ask me . . . since I was the oldest, the natural thing would have been . . . for me to go out and work fulltime and help them with the family. But they didn't [ask me to].

All of the migrant parents (about one-fourth of the subjects) had made the sacrifice of settling down in one place, stopping their migrant patterns, when they realized it was having a negative impact on their children's schooling. In some cases this was a particularly difficult decision for families when there were no guarantees of steady work. Some fathers would leave the family behind, while they continued the migrant work on their own. For one subject, a lawyer and community organizer, the family's decision to settle in the Napa Valley was especially fortuitous. Apparently, teachers took note of the family's sacrifice for the education of their son and made an extra effort on his behalf:

> We were one of the only families that stayed. . . . I was the only
> [Chicano] who stayed [in school] after the grape picking. So, the
> teacher took a half hour every day away from the other kids to teach
> me English. That made a lot of difference.

For another subject, who would end up being a physician, the family's
decision to stop migrating, was the clear turning point in his educational
career:

> [W]hen I was in the seventh grade, they were going to keep me back
> because I was failing. And my brother had failed the year before and
> the family didn't want us to fail. That was a major decision that was
> made, that we no longer migrate during the school year . . . from the
> seventh to the eighth grade I went from a D and F student to an
> honor student.

PARENTAL ASPIRATIONS

The literature on achievement motivation also suggests that the parents of
high-performing students usually have high aspirations for their children and
transmit these aspirations to them. This literature, however, is based for the
most part on middle-class samples. LeVine (1974), in an analysis of parental
goals in cross-cultural context, suggested that

> In populations with relatively scarce or precarious resources for
> subsistence, parents will have as their overriding conscious concern
> the child's capacity for future economic self-maintenance (broadly
> defined), particularly after his survival seems assured; and child-
> rearing customs will reflect this priority. (p. 231)

The experiences of the subjects of this study reflect this analysis to a large
degree. More than half of the parents, both mothers and fathers, were believed
by the subjects to aspire to nothing higher than a high school education for
their children (see table 2.4).

For many of these parents, high school graduation was a high goal that
they believed would assure their children a reasonable livelihood in the future.
In response to the question "How far do you think your mother hoped you
would go in school?" a physician who grew up in a migrant family commented,

> High school. She knew that if I graduated from high school, I could
> get a good job after I got out. Because at that time . . . she grew up in
> a time when high school graduation was the goal to attain, and once
> you had achieved that . . . you were really, you know, you were
> somebody.

Table 2.4. *Parental Aspirations*

Mother

	Less than High School	High School	Some College	College Graduate	Graduate Professional Education	Technical Education	Don't Know	Total N
TOTAL	2 (4%)	17 (34%)	3 (6%)	12 (24%)	8 (16%)	0 (0%)	8 (16%)	50 (100%)
GENDER								
Male	1 (3%)	12 (40%)	2 (7%)	6 (20%)	6 (20%)	0 (0%)	3 (10%)	30 (100%)
Female	1 (5%)	5 (25%)	1 (5%)	6 (30%)	2 (10%)	0 (0%)	5 (25%)	20 (100%)
DEGREE								
J.D.	1 (8%)	2 (17%)	1 (8%)	4 (33%)	3 (25%)	0 (0%)	1 (8%)	12 (100%)
M.D.	1 (9%)	4 (40%)	1 (9%)	4 (33%)	1 (8%)	0 (0%)	1 (9%)	12 (100%)
Ph.D.	0 (0%)	11 (42%)	1 (4%)	4 (15%)	4 (15%)	0 (0%)	6 (23%)	26 (100%)

Father

	Less than High School	High School	Some College	College Graduate	Graduate Professional Education	Technical Education	Don't Know	Total N
TOTAL	7 (15%)	13 (33%)	2 (5%)	9 (21%)	5 (10%)	0 (0%)	9 (15%)	45 (100%)
GENDER								
Male	4 (16%)	8 (32%)	2 (8%)	4 (16%)	3 (12%)	0 (0%)	4 (16%)	25 (100%)
Female	3 (16%)	5 (26%)	0 (0%)	5 (26%)	2 (11%)	0 (0%)	5 (26%)	20 (100%)
DEGREE								
J.D.	2 (18%)	2 (18%)	0 (0%)	3 (27%)	2 (18%)	0 (0%)	2 (18%)	11 (100%)
M.D.	1 (9%)	5 (45%)	1 (9%)	2 (18%)	1 (9%)	0 (0%)	1 (9%)	11 (100%)
Ph.D.	4 (17%)	6 (27%)	1 (4%)	4 (18%)	2 (9%)	0 (0%)	6 (28%)	23 (100%)

Whether parents' aspirations for their children were at the level of high school graduation, or extended to a college education, it is interesting to note that levels of aspiration were relatively similar for both sons and daughters with respect to encouraging college attendance. Where this differed was in the smaller percentages of parents who envisioned a graduate or professional education for their daughters. That is, they did not tend to suggest that their daughters should be doctors, lawyers, or scientists in the way they did for their sons. Also, there were considerably more daughters than sons who did not know what their fathers had envisioned for them. Hence, overall support for education was relatively similar for both males and females within the family, but parents tended to set more specific (and somewhat higher) goals for their sons.

PARENTING STYLE

There was no clear preference for an authoritative style of parenting among the parents of these subjects. Only about one-third of both mothers and fathers were viewed by their children as exhibiting the style the research suggests should have been important in fostering academic aspirations. Contrary to the bulk of the literature on this topic, parents were reported to exhibit a wide variety of parenting styles.[1] As might be expected, the most common style was authoritarian, with more fathers than mothers falling into this category. One can only speculate that, like many other family process variables, the effects of parenting style may be highly dependent upon an interaction with other family attributes. For example, we could hypothesize that the negative effects of an authoritarian or overly permissive style of parenting may be attenuated in a circumstance in which, due to privation, the subject must exercise great autonomy in taking on work and family responsibilities at an early age.

Moreover, the necessity for parents to exercise greater control in environments where children can fall easy prey to an oppositional street culture

---

1. Parenting styles were elicited by first introducing the subjects to the basic concepts in the literature with the following statement:

It has been suggested that there are three basic styles of discipline that parents use: authoritarian, in which the parent is very strict, makes decisions without consulting others, doesn't usually go back on those decisions, and doesn't usually attempt to explain them; authoritative, in which the parent may exert strong discipline, but usually attempts to provide a rationale for decisions, a reason "why" the decision was made. The parent may also include the child in the decision-making. And permissive, in which the parent frequently allows the child to make decisions which affect the child.

Subjects were then asked to reflect on the way their parents usually interacted with them and to comment on how such guidance or discipline was administered, first by their mothers, then by their fathers.

must be taken into account. Clark (1983), McLeod (1987), and McLaren (1994) all describe in ethnographic detail the ways in which poor and minority children in the inner cities find themselves marginalized by school and outside the sphere of family influence; they sound a common theme of loss of parental control and subsequent failure in school. Hence, to some extent, "democratic" parenting styles may be a risky luxury that some poor, minority parents with high aspirations for their children may feel they can ill afford.

PARENT INVOLVEMENT

Finally, recent research has turned up consistently high correlations between parent involvement in schools and the academic performance of students (Moles, 1982). Although the causal direction has not been firmly established, the assumption is that greater parent involvement leads to higher academic achievement in children. Given the high degree of interest that most of these parents exhibited in their children's education, did they involve themselves in the schools that their children attended?

None of the fifty subjects described their parents as being active in their schools. A very few mentioned that their parents occasionally attended a PTA meeting, but for the most part, these parents kept a fair distance from the schools, unless a problem occurred, and this was likely to result in a visit to the school. The following response to the question of whether his parents ever visited his school to check on his progress was typical of the way most people interpreted their parents' lack of school involvement:

> [My parents visited] only because they were forced to, I think. They .
> . . my mother . . . would not go, I think mainly because she didn't
> feel up to presenting herself and trying to communicate with the
> teachers whom I guess obviously she held in high esteem. And
> maybe she didn't feel like she would be able to talk to them,
> although she knew how to speak, although at that time it was
> probably broken . . . I think they were always interested but that
> held them back.

Some assumptions about social class, cultural capital, and parents' effects on their children's schooling that are drawn from the research literature may also be unfounded. For example, Lareau's (1989) depiction of the vast differences between middle- and working-class parents and the cultural capital they have available to expend *within* the school may suggest an overly narrow interpretation of the possibilities of parental involvement and its effect on schooling. Low-status parents may, in fact, have considerable cultural capital of the sort valued by the schools; however, in a society with racist tendencies, this may not always be evident to school personnel. As noted earlier, the majority of these parents shared many of the attitudes and dispositions that make up the cultural capital of the middle and upper classes: they were literate and held a high value for various forms of literacy, and they supported the aims of the school and nurtured their children's aspirations. Yet they would no doubt have been viewed by the schools, like most poor parents, as in need of "parent education." These unequal encounters between parents, teachers, and administrators can serve to reinforce the school's perception that the students are "disadvantaged" by their parents' limited formal educations, and can leave the parents feeling hostile and embarrassed. The best strategy may sometimes be for parents to support the school's mission from a distance. Greater contact between parents and schools does not necessarily breed better understanding.

Parents of these subjects did not interact very frequently with the schools, but they used their cultural capital to reinforce the mission of the schools, a mission that they shared, from within the home. This argues for a different model of "parent involvement" than that which is typically seen in schools, and a broader construction of the concept of cultural capital. Contact between parents and schools, when such encounters occur between individuals perceived to hold equal status, can no doubt be beneficial to students. Considerable evidence exists to confirm this, notably in such programs as described by Comer (1988) and Delgado-Gaitan (1991). However, there is no reason to believe that low-income, minority students will gain any advantage from "parent involvement" that lacks reciprocity and serves solely to transmit information that the schools think is important, shape the behaviors of the parent, or allow the parent the opportunity to provide a service to the school. Moreover, in a study drawn from the National Educational Longitudinal Study (NELS) database on eighth-grade students, Peng and Lee (1991, in Wang, Haertel, & Walberg, 1994) found that direct parental involvement and assistance are not as important as the availability of learning opportunities, frequent parent-child conversations, and higher education expectations. Data from the current study appear to confirm those findings.

SUMMARY OF HOME INFLUENCES

While parents of these subjects did many of the things described in the literature as promoting high academic achievement among the middle and upper classes, including providing opportunities for their children to develop a sense of self-efficacy, supporting their educational goals, and setting high standards, they also differed in important ways that call into question some deeply held beliefs about student achievement.

Although there is substantial evidence that smaller family size and family intactness are positively correlated with increased academic achievement, the subjects in this study came from very large families, averaging more than five siblings, and fully one quarter came from families that had been disrupted by death, divorce, or abandonment. Moreover they consistently reported that their siblings were a great resource to them in achieving their academic goals. Siblings served as role models and counselors, and even when similar opportunities had been closed to older brothers and sisters, they supported and encouraged the subjects' aspirations. A recent study of Southeast Asian students reports similar findings, raising a question about the extent to which previous research findings have been blind to variations in family dynamics across different cultures.

There has long been a consensus in the psychology and child development literature that a particular parenting style is most commonly associated with high academic achievement. Baumrind (1989) refers to this style as authoritative, and it is characterized by warm, firm, but democratic guidance. This parenting style is believed to foster a sense of self-efficacy and independent goal-setting. Parents of these subjects, however, were seldom described as authoritative. These parents, and especially the fathers, were most frequently characterized as "authoritarian," a style of parenting believed to promote excessive dependence and to undermine children's self-concepts. Two issues are raised by these contradictory findings: the extent to which interpretations of parenting styles may be culturally mediated (that is, does authoritarianism represent the same things across different cultures and social circumstances), and the extent to which past research has failed to consider adequately the social contexts in which parenting occurs.

Finally, the research on parent involvement in schools is consistent in finding positive correlations between parent involvement (however defined) and children's academic achievement. While this research is virtually all correlational, schools have treated the findings as causal, rushing to create parent involvement programs in an effort to increase student achievement. Parents of these high-achieving subjects, however, had very little contact with schools and seldom, if ever, spoke with their children's teachers. Nonetheless, they supported the goals of the school at home, helped with homework when they could, and instilled high standards in their children. One could argue that their children's case would not have been helped, and in fact could have been hurt, by greater parental contact with the schools. Having no contact with these parents, teachers were denied the opportunity to form judgments about students' potential based on their parents' limited education or ability to communicate in English. School personnel had no option but to accept the children at face value, as the high performers that they typically were. As Clark (1983) concludes, "parents influence learning through enforcement of normative standards, and by the specific behaviors which contribute directly to learning" (p. 155), and this occurs in the home, not in the school.

Thus, schools may be well advised to review their assumptions about parent involvement and school achievement, and focus instead on creating environments where the real needs of families can be met, such as the sewing room, equipped with donated material and sewing machines, where low-income parents can come to sew clothes for their children (cf. Gándara, 1992). In these contexts, where the primary contacts are informal and nonevaluative, parents may see the school as an ally rather than an adversary. Even so, not all parents will come, but it should not be assumed that they do not care or that they lack interest, or even the skills, to support their children's schooling.

THREE

Family Stories as Cultural Capital

Folklorists have long understood the power of stories to transmit group and family beliefs, attitudes, aspirations, and self-images. Family stories, in particular, often serve to "provide the family with esteem because they often show family members in an attractive light or define the family in a flattering way. They also give messages and instructions; they offer blueprints and ideals . . . " (Stone, 1988, p. 5). They may even serve as a vehicle of social mobility.

Grebler, Moore, and Guzmán (1970), in their seminal study of Mexican Americans, noted, in passing, a phenomenon which was also prominent among the subjects in this study. In the interviews they conducted, they found a frequent recounting of family stories that

> suggested that some kind of "myth of the golden past" (in this case, family past) might play a role in social mobility. Such men often reported one of their parents or grandparents as coming from well-to-do families in Mexico, but having lost status through gambling, misalliance, or other personal problems . . . (p. 337)

Similarly, when these subjects were asked to describe the reasons their parents gave for the migration of their family to the United States, some such "myth" would often be a part of the recounting of that migratory experience. More than half of the sample offered, without prompting, that one or the other of their parents, but most often the mother, was said to have come from a family that was highly esteemed in Mexico. Many of the stories fit the category that folklorists refer to as "lost fortune stories." Such stories serve a special function in the lives of people who find themselves in diminished or demeaning circumstances. They are "useful first, because [they] establish family worth—and hence individual worth—by reference to an apocryphal fortune that the family used to have, and second, because [they] testify to the blamelessness of the current generation in the loss of that fortune—'they' lost it, they are responsible" (Stone, 1988, p. 156).

51

One example of such a story was told by a lawyer, son of a copper-miner father and a mother with a seventh-grade education, as he recounted the stories his mother told him as a child:

My grandfather's family—[my mother's] father—were landowners . . . and she describes things like how my grandfather used to hide the jewelry and hide the valuables, and stuff like that . . . [and] they had orchards...[but] my grandfather was dispossessed of his share . . . he was an outcast from the family and because of the difference in status between my grandfather and my grandmother . . . he was never welcome in the family any more . . . that's when they came here.

In this story, wealth and status are lost not through any real fault of the ancestor but because he fell in love with someone of lower class standing. The story at once relieves his descendants of any blame for their own diminished circumstances and creates a powerful statement about the intrinsic worth of people independent of their social status.

Another story of the lost fortune type was told by the psychologist whose mother had raised him, and his brothers, as a single parent:

[My mother told us] how her grandfather was like a multimillionaire type. He was a genius in the mines. And none of that went down to her family because of wills and stuff like that. And they were always very proud because her uncles owned a hotel in Aguas Calientes, and that was something nice back there, even though we don't have it here. [She would say,] "You know you can hold your head up high." And we never believed it. We always thought she was just making it all up.

Again, the ancestor in this story exemplifies values to be emulated, but he also posesses an important, and perhaps heritable, characteristic: he was not only wealthy, he was "a genius."

Not all of the family fortunes were lost, however. Some stories included elements of the present: the idea that the family in Mexico is still quite prosperous and remains as tangible evidence of the family's inherent status. Seldom had subjects ever had contact with these illustrious family members in Mexico, however, and the tales remained as unconfirmed legends in their minds. A Chicana physician recounted this story of her family's fortunes:

My father, if he had stayed in Mexico . . . would have done a different kind of job. . . . In their family a cousin has a wine thing. My father would have had a different life in Mexico. It would probably have not been labor. . . . My mother's family, also in Mexico, they were more into the mercantile and they ended up having stores. They have huge stores, that kind of thing. . . . Coming here . . . meant labor.

Another variant on the family fortune stories was one in which the family had achieved great prestige in Mexico, or high levels of education. A political scientist told how his mother had impressed upon him that her family was well educated, and she, too, would have had such opportunities but for the fact that she was a woman and had been the victim of her husband's misfortunes. Although the brothers she described were her own contemporaries, the subject had never met them:

> In her family [mother's], some were farmers, others were politicians and became very high officials in the Mexican government, including one who became a congressman, one became an attorney. These were her brothers.

A similar type of story, but with a different twist, was told by a woman who would first become a nurse, then a psychologist once she realized that she did not have to remain in a "woman's job."

> She [subject's mother] always said how smart I was and how with her relatives there was a lot of brilliance, and we were fifth-generation people and still had a chance to get the genes from the ancestor who used to be governor . . . and who negotiated with Washington . . . she would always emphasize that she had been told by someone who had traced her roots that you could inherit these things even to the fifth generation. So there was a lot of instilling in us that we were bright people.

A particularly Mexican story has to do with the change in political fortunes associated with the Mexican Revolution. Many subjects had stories of ancestors who had made a quick retreat north of the border because of their alliance with the losing side in the Revolution. Of course, this hasty departure always meant a loss of status and financial well-being. A lawyer, whose parents continued to echo political themes through nightly discussions of social justice and labor organizing, recounted the stories he had heard of the prestigious political posts his ancestors had held prior to the Revolution:

> My grandfather was like a sort of judge of the town, [and] my mother's father's brother—therefore her uncle—was mayor of a town in Sonora and was politically active. My mother's father was also politically active . . . he was in the losing party, so he had to leave town real fast and that's when they came across the border.

As Grebler, Moore, and Guzmán (1970) indicate, "there simply were not enough middle class and well-to-do families [in Mexico] to accommodate this many ancestors" (p. 338) within their sample. Likewise, one wonders at the extent to which the family myths in this sample were embellished in the retelling.

Whether the family stories are true, in either a general or specific way, is probably less important than that they were so salient, so much a part of the subjects' perceptions of themselves, and their families, that they came easily to mind without prodding.

What is also notable about the stories is that they are almost always told by women, by the mothers to their children, whether the story is about her family or her husband's, it is she who communicates this information. The reader will also recall that it was the mothers who played the largest role in supporting their children's academic aspirations. Could it be that the stories were a form of cultural capital, an explicit means of passing on middle class attitudes and dispositions about self-worth, competence, and hopefulness from one generation to another?

In a related sense, the stories may have served to establish a "folk theory" of success which could compete with the more dismal belief system to which these subjects would be exposed within their own communities. As Ogbu and Matute-Bianchi (1986) contend:

> Every society or population has its own theory of getting ahead; and each folk theory tends to generate its own ideal behaviors and its own ideal successful persons or role models—the kinds of people who are widely perceived by members of the population as people who are successful or people who can get ahead because of their personal attributes and behaviors. Parents usually try to raise their children to be like these people, and as children grow older they, too, strive to be like them. (p. 84)

If Ogbu and Matute-Bianchi are correct, however, it must be a particular challenge for parents raising children in low-income minority communities to come up with appropriate role models for their children. It may be necessary to create their own conceptions of what such people would be like. The family stories can serve this function. These stories, then, can provide not only models of people who have made it, but they may also engender in children a sense of hopefulness which might otherwise be absent in their lives. For as McLeod (1987) notes, "of all the factors contributing to social reproduction (e.g., tracking, social relations of schooling, class-based differences in linguistic codes), regulation of aspirations is perhaps the most important" (p. 21). Hence, the most critical intervention the parent can make to break a cycle of low achievement is the alteration of aspirations and the introduction of a sense of hopefulness based on tangible evidence of "people like us" who make it.

According to Bandura (1990), one of the four principle ways in which children develop a "self-belief of efficacy," that is, the strength and determination to persevere in face of obstacles and sometimes even rejection, is through *modeling*. "The models in people's lives serve as sources of interest, inspiration, and skills . . . Seeing people similar to oneself succeed by sustained effort raises the observers' beliefs about their own efficacy" (p. 327).

It seems logical, then, that the stories were a way for mothers to convey to their children that the current circumstance in which they lived—poverty— was not one in which they needed remain. In fact, one might construe, it was atypical for their family, a fluke of sorts that could be remedied. The stories point to a great deal of hopefulness in the families of these subjects, the same kind of hopefulness that so powerfully distinguished the school-oriented "Brothers" from the "Hallway Hangers" who had rejected schooling in McLeod's study. The stories kept alive a dream of what they once were and what they could be again.

As Pierre Bourdieu, the French sociologist, has noted, "academic performance is linked to cultural background . . . and is more strongly related to parents' educational history than to parents' occupational status" (Swartz, 1977, p. 547). The family stories, then, represented the *creation* of a history that would break the links between the parents' current occupational status and their children's future academic attainment. In this sense, the family stories represent the clearest form of cultural capital, for through the telling of the stories, the mothers transmitted the cultural values and dispositions which Bourdieu posits as being the powerful mediating factor between schooling and social class.

The pervasiveness of the phenomenon of family stories of lost fortunes and of illustrious ancestors and extended family members is so great among this sample that it cannot be ignored in attempting to explain the origins of their extraordinary aspirations. This is particularly so in light of the fact that these individuals sought not only to improve their own situation but to challenge an elite culture, that of academia, which is among the most difficult for low-status individuals to penetrate.

FOUR

Schools and Neighborhoods

Both schools and neighborhoods have an effect on student achievement, albeit a smaller effect than that of families. A major problem in the research on school and neighborhood effects, however, has been the difficulty in separating one from the other. Even the most carefully controlled studies have suffered, to some extent, from the problem of drawing a definitive line between variation in achievement that can be attributed to the school a student attends and that which can be attributed to the neighborhood in which the student, and the school, reside (Jencks & Mayer, 1990). Nonetheless, a great deal of research has been conducted, especially on the effects of schools, and we now turn to that research to help shed light on the experiences of the fifty individuals in this study.

In spite of the finding that schools account for only a small portion of the variance in student performance (Coleman et al., 1966; Jencks et al, 1972; Averch et al., 1974), the *particular* school a student attends can have important effects on his or her achievement (Hanushek, 1989). Studies have found consistent correlations between the socioeconomic composition of schools and the achievement aspirations of their graduating seniors (Levine, Mitchell, & Havighurst, 1970; Jencks & Mayer, 1990). However, even when socio-economic status and family background characteristics of students were con-trolled, Mortimore et al. (1988) found substantial differences among schools for both cognitive and noncognitive pupil outcomes. The original Coleman et al. report, *Equality of Educational Opportunity* (1966), also noted that schools had a greater effect on minority student achievement than they did on the achievement of white students.

Two major studies which have investigated the effects of public versus private schools, both concluded that Catholic schools with their shared sense of community and high academic standards, even for minority students, had a more positive effect on student achievement than did socioeconomically similar public schools that appeared to lack these characteristics (Coleman & Hoffer, 1987; Bryk, Lee, & Holland, 1993).

Schools can be viewed as having three major elements which affect school performance: teachers, student body, and curriculum. While large-scale quantitative studies have had difficulty isolating the specific effects of teachers, according to Hanushek "there are striking differences in average gain in student achievement across teachers" (1989, p.48). Perhaps the best evidence of teacher behaviors associated with student achievement comes from studies of effective schools and effective teaching. In this literature, there is a consistent finding that both classrooms and schools that enjoy exceptionally high achievement are characterized by teachers who hold high academic standards and expectations for all of their students (Purkey & Smith, 1983; Lucas, Henze, & Donato, 1990).

Coleman et al. (1966) also concluded that the composition of the student body accounted for most of the achievement effects which were attributable to schools in their study. Others have pursued this question with similar results (Winkler, 1975). In related work, Oakes (1985) has demonstrated that the curriculum track, and hence the immediate peer group with which a student is placed, can have a major effect on that student's schooling experience, likelihood of dropping out, and future life chances. Hence, there is ample evidence that curriculum tracking and the peers available within the school make a difference in the achievement of students.

There is also substantial evidence that minority students who attend primarily minority—racially and ethnically isolated—schools do not perform as well as those minority students who attend more racially integrated schools (Coleman et al., 1966; Carter, 1970; Orfield & Paul, 1988; Jencks & Mayer, 1990). Much of the difference in achievement in these schools has been attributed to the fact that they tend to be funded more poorly and to have less-experienced and less-able teachers (Carter, 1970; Carter and Segura, 1979; Educational Testing Service, 1991). However, both the research reviewed and the experiences of the subjects of this study suggest that the internal dynamics of naturally desegregated schools may also differ from those of racially isolated schools in their effect on student achievement, at least for Chicano students.

IMPORTANCE OF PARTICULAR SCHOOLS

Certainly these subjects and their families believed that schools made a difference, for many made conscious efforts to get into schools that they considered "better." One woman, the daughter of an itinerant musician who had never attended school himself, commented on her father's decision to move the family out of the barrio in which they lived in order to gain access to a better school for his children:

> My father decided to definitely move out of the barrio, and the reason he did was because the one thing that had been strong in my

father was the desire to get a strong education and he was very concerned that we would not get an education in the barrio...and that is why we had to get out.

Neighborhood effects were also confounded with school effects for some subjects who lived in areas of the barrio that provided better schooling options. It is unclear whether these parents were aware of the options when they chose their place of residence, however, this is a common phenomenon among the middle class. Many subjects commented on how important they felt the particular schools they attended were in shaping their academic futures. A young man who went on to finish his law degree at an Ivy League college mused:

> I have sometimes asked myself . . . whether or not I would have achieved as much, or even more, if I had gone to that [the barrio] school. . . . But I don't know. I knew that in going to an Anglo high school I was going to have to overcome everything that I was carrying with me which was going to keep me from achieving it. I did it. Having done it gave me an incredible amount of confidence and completely convinced me that I could do anything I wanted to.

Another subject, when asked what was critically different about his background that might have contributed to his high aspirations, replied:

> That I went to Catholic school. It was head and shoulders different from public schools. My friends in Catholic school and I, we were proud of who we were. We had pride. We knew that we were studying hard compared to all those other guys that don't carry any books home. . . . We felt like we were doing something. . . . I don't know what would have happened to me if I'd gone to public school. Maybe I would have surfaced, maybe, but I don't know.

Of course, most subjects did not go to Catholic schools. For many of them, the experiences they had in particular public schools were believed to have made a difference. A political scientist whose older sister had invited him to live with her and her husband so that he could attend an upper-middle-class, mostly white school, reviewed that experience:

> I could have stayed at Ravenswood High School, and I would not have gone on to college. And I also think that if I had stayed in the old neighborhood, I would not have gone on to college. But the experience that I had at Campbell, in particular, sort of began to provide me with that proper tone of work, to create a situation in which I could go to college.

Another subject, a physician, found the change of schools he made early in his academic career to be fortuitous in the way it resulted in a different opinion of himself:

> I went to Marengo. That was the first school I went to. There I don't remember being at the top of the class. . . . I was kind of right in the middle, average. When I went to Murchison, all of sudden I was at the top of the class . . . and they tested us once and found that about three of us who were transferred from this other school . . . they found we were doing third-grade level. I always thought, gee, that was interesting. Here I was in the middle of my class and suddenly at this school, I'm smart. I'm one of the smart guys. . . . [Then] I remember going to an Open House and my instructor told my parents that I was "college material" . . . and it seems from then on, I was their son: "college material."

Drawing on a number of other studies, Jencks and Mayer (1990) explain the phenomenon experienced by the physician above with reference to the metaphor of the campus as a frog pond. They cite research showing that while attending a school in which peers have high aspirations can positively affect college plans, attending a school with a high socioeconomic status, and hence high scoring peers, does not increase one's chances of going on to higher education. In other words, it is helpful to be inspired by highly motivated classmates, but some of the benefit is lost if this results in having to compete with students who are also high scorers. Our physician was fortunate to find himself in a school where the teachers held him in high esteem, and where his peers did not outshine him.

CURRICULUM TRACKING

Almost all of the study subjects were eventually tracked into college-preparatory courses when they were in high school; however, for many it was a battle to get there. At one time or another 30 percent of the subjects were either placed in, or slated for, vocational or general education curriculum tracks. The likelihood is that, had they not ultimately been placed in the college-preparatory track, they would never have achieved the level of education that they eventually did (Oakes, 1985). These subjects were astute enough, in most cases, to be painfully aware of this fact. Many complained that they had to fight for the right to take college-prep courses; the schools frequently did not identify them as being "college material."

A lawyer, who had come to the United States in the fourth grade recounted how difficult it was to get out of a lower track once she had been placed in one:

[W]hen I went to the tenth grade, I took that special stupid test they give you and it came out that I would have been a fantastic mechanic . . . so they tracked me average [again] which precluded me from taking college-prep classes, and I had already taken geometry and Spanish and biology and some other courses in junior high. Now that I was tracked, and they tracked me secretarial, I used to take my electives as college-prep courses. It didn't get to the eleventh grade until they finally tracked me into what they called the college prep, that I could take the classes that I wanted. So I was taking these stupid homemaking, which I always hated, typing, which I always hated, courses that I didn't like.

Many subjects indicted their high school counselors for placing them in vocational and non-college-preparatory tracks, in spite of their good achievement in school. Some subjects interpreted this as an expression of racism:

My first day signing up [at high school] . . . my dad had been out working in the fields, but he came home early this day to take me so I could get registered . . . there was a counselor. . . . And I took my eighth-grade diploma which was straight A's, and I was valedictorian of my eighth grade. . . . And I told him I would like to go to college and could he fit me into college-prep classes? And he looked at my grades and everything, and said, well, he wasn't sure I could handle it. My dad didn't understand. He was there with me. And this counselor put me in non-college-prep classes. I remember going home and feeling just terrible.

In some cases, subjects were dogged by test scores or impressions that were very difficult to overcome. The following example is illustrative of a number of individuals in the sample.

My counselors didn't come to me and say we are putting you on a special tracking upwards because you are doing so well, but rather it was something I was entitled to and I was aware that I could go in and ask for it. In fact sometimes I had to insist on it and much later I found out why. Apparently one of the reasons my counselors had such a negative image of me and why they were always insisting I was not college material was because I have always done extremely poorly on IQ exams. And they were totally locked into that IQ . . . like 94, 95, 96 . . . and they never explained why I was doing so well academically when my IQ test was so low.

One subject, who was later to become an acclaimed scientist, was so disturbed by his encounter with a counselor that he counted that incident as perhaps the seminal experience that propelled him to higher education:

I was in an accelerated class, I was in the top 10 percent of my high school graduating class. I wasn't dumb; I was pretty good, I thought. She [the counselor] told me, "Well, you should go into vocational school." I got so mad with that woman, and it was primarily based on some damned exam that I took . . . and I don't believe in exams anyway . . . she was, I think, the one who motivated me to go to university because she told me I shouldn't go. So I thought, "Well, the hell with you!"

Once subjects were placed into the college-prep track, it had an enormous impact on them, not only in that they were given classes that would lead to college, but in the new peer group it defined for them. In virtually every case, they became one of only a small handful of (and often they were the only) Chicanos in their academic peer group. This had a number of consequences.

The very Mexican-looking son of farmworkers, who became student body president of his mostly Anglo school, described his experience at being tracked in this way:

[T]hey put me in a group that kind of restricted who I really hung around with, because it was always the people who were the smarter kids. And the smarter kids were always the people, you know, who were from the higher socioeconomic group . . . and always, you know, the white kids . . . the principal's son, another teacher's daughter. And it kind of restricted my association with the other people in my class . . . by the courses you take you kind of restrict yourself . . . who you even communicate with.

Another subject, also the daughter of farmworkers, described the peer group that was created for her by her college prep classes:

In high school, I tended to hang around with kids who were in my class. And since they had tracking, some of my friends from the migrant labor camps did not get put into the higher tracks. So, I knew them in the labor camp, I would talk to them, they were my friends . . . but I would never see them in my classes, and I would rarely see them even in school. The ones I hung out with in school were the studious ones, most of them in my class. Those are the ones I had homework to discuss with.

DESEGREGATED SCHOOLS

The reason that the study subjects were in a position to be tracked into classes that were typically all-white was because they overwhelmingly attended desegregated or mostly Anglo schools. In both elementary and high school, between 60 and 70 percent of the subjects reported that they attended mostly white (and usually middle to upper-middle class) or mixed schools in which *at least* half of the students were Anglo (see table 4.1). Even at elementary school, where school populations tend to more accurately reflect the racial and economic character of the local neighborhood, only one-third of the subjects attended mostly Chicano schools. Attendance in mostly white and desegregated schools had enormous consequences, not only for the curriculum these subjects were offered, but for the peers to whom they were exposed.

Inasmuch as these subjects came from poor families and lived in poor neighborhoods in the Southwest, where segregation of Chicanos is typical (Donato, Menchaca, & Valencia, 1991), what accounted for the fact that these subjects attended the kinds of schools that they did? One explanation lies in a fact of life for farmworkers. Those children of farmworkers who attend school often go to the same schools as the well-off sons and daughters of the large landowners for whom their parents work. In the early grades this results in highly mixed schools, but as the students move into high school, large proportions of farmworker children drop out, resulting in secondary schools that are often largely white, middle-class enclaves.

Catholic schools can also provide an integrated education experience for low-income, minority students. For a few of the students, this clearly was the case. However, only about one-third of the subjects had attended parochial schools for three or more years. Seventy percent were educated by the public schools.

There is another explanation for this disproportionately large sample of people who attended highly integrated and mostly white schools. This was the phenomenon of students, themselves, making the decision to attend schools outside their neighborhoods. Several subjects commented that they were acutely aware of the differences in opportunities that existed between schools, and they made the choices about which schools they would attend. The following is an explanation given by a young man who lived on the boundary between two very distinct schools:

> When I graduated from junior high the big question was which of the two high schools was I going to choose. And the reason why the choice was important was because Lincoln was predominantly, 95 percent, Mexican American and that's where most of the kids from my junior high school were going. . . . Franklin, at that time, was 99 percent Anglo. And the choice was very critical at that point primarily because it was a choice of following the rest of the crowd. . . . I was involved in gangs when I was in junior high school . . . most of them had been arrested for one reason or another. . . . My decision

Table 4.1. *High School Racial/Ethnic Composition*

	All/ Almost All Mexican American	Mostly Minority (Black, Mexican American, etc.)	Mostly Minority Excluding Mexican American	Mostly Mexican American; Significant Number of Anglos	Mostly Anglo	Mixed*	Total N
TOTAL	8 (16%)	2 (4%)	1 (2%)	5 (10%)	25 (50%)	9 (18%)	50 (100%)
GENDER							
Male	4 (13%)	1 (3%)	1 (3%)	5 (17%)	13 (43%)	6 (20%)	30 (100%)
Female	4 (20%)	1 (5%)	0 (0%)	0 (0%)	12 (60%)	3 (15%)	20 (100%)
DEGREE							
J.D.	1 (8%)	0 (0%)	1 (8%)	1 (8%)	7 (50%)	2 (17%)	12 (100%)
M.D.	3 (25%)	1 (8%)	0 (0%)	1 (9%)	4 (33%)	3 (25%)	12 (100%)
Ph.D.	4 (15%)	1 (4%)	0 (0%)	3 (12%)	14 (54%)	4 (15%)	26 (100%)

*At least 50 percent Anglo or more than half of schooling experience took place in mostly Anglo schools.

was to go to Franklin. . . . I knew the only way to escape this was to disassociate myself from all of them by going to a high school where they weren't going.

Another subject talked about how his schooling was shaped by his two older brothers who had decided that they wouldn't go to school in the barrio where they lived:

My two brothers were trying to do well. They wanted to go to college, that's why they left the barrio, they didn't want to go to the schools there, the public schools especially . . . they found a Catholic high school through a friend of theirs, and that's where the whole movement started. We used to get out, take the bus across town.

When their mother suggested that the Catholic high school was too expensive and she couldn't afford the one they had selected, and suggested an alternative school, the boys replied:

"It's not good enough, look at all those guys, they're not going anywhere." They saw the writing on the wall. Pretty perceptive, actually.

A final explanation may lie in the conscious choices made by the parents to move to neighborhoods that would provide better school experiences for their children. Grebler, Moore, and Guzmán (1970) described Mexican American communities in Texas and California as breaking down into different types. One type was the "frontier" community where the more upwardly mobile Chicanos tended to locate on the fringes of the white community. In the Grebler et al. study, frontier communities were usually ethnically mixed, which was not as typically the case for the communities from which these subjects came. Nonetheless they seemed to share similar characteristics in that they were usually the "better" Mexican communities located on the fringes of white neighborhoods. It is reasonable to hypothesize that many of these hardworking, upwardly mobile Chicano families had realized the social and educational advantages that would accrue to their children as a result of living in "frontier" areas. Many subjects, in fact, talked about living "on the school boundary line" or "the other side of the ditch" from the really bad neighborhood. Typical of the comments many subjects made about their neighborhoods were these reflections of a sociology professor who grew up near the border in California:

My neighborhood was a little bit poorer than the average . . . [but] people were real conscious that the barrio was the lowest and where I was from was the second lowest . . . we didn't have sidewalks and things like that. The school next to us . . . was like 95 percent

Chicanos. Like I said, we were on the border between the barrio which is a "real barrio" and our neighborhood which is a mix. The barrio had a reputation for a lot of fights. It was a rough neighborhood. It's no accident that we didn't live in that neighborhood.

Most subjects grew up in urban areas or small towns where the majority of their neighbors were other Chicano families (see table 4.2). Yet they went to schools where the student composition was very different from that of their neighborhoods. Later, in the discussion of peer relationships, we will see that this fact was very important in shaping their identities and fostering a value for multiple peer groups.

One young woman who grew up in Southern California, and later became a physician, spoke for many of the subjects in the following commentary:

I went to schools where I wasn't the norm, but we lived in neighborhoods where we were. In Barstow, where I was districted in a different, more prosperous elementary school, I wasn't the norm in school, but I lived in a neighborhood where we were. Even in New Mexico, the same way.

MENTORS IN SCHOOL AND OUT

A cursory review of the literature on mentoring in education yields one very strong impression: there is little consensus among scholars on the definition of mentoring or the characteristics of the mentoring relationship (Jacobi, 1991). For some (Muskal & Carlquist, 1992), it may range from a single motivating conversation to a life-long relationship. Bloom (1985) identifies different types of mentorship, depending on the stage of development of the mentee; and Gage and Berliner (1991) contend that the mentoring relationship must be one of mutual benefit which takes place in the context of some kind of work. The only things that all these definitions share in common are the notions that the relationship of the participants must be one of superior and subordinate and the career of the subordinate is advanced through this relationship.

In this study, mentoring was defined as a process by which a particular individual dramatically affected the orientation to schooling of the subject. The mentor was the person who encouraged, showed the way, and nurtured the aspirations of the subject to pursue higher education. While most subjects reported that they had had positive experiences with teachers who encouraged them, only half of the subjects actually nominated a teacher or other person outside of the family as a real mentor. Though many of the study subjects were highly critical of counselors with whom they had contact in high school, just as many commented on the extraordinarily positive role that some

Table 4.2. *Neighborhood Composition*

	90% + Mexican American	Mixed Minorities	Mostly Mexican American Significant Number of Anglos	Mostly Minorities Excluding Mexican American	Mixed Ethnicities	Mostly Anglo	Total N
TOTAL	25 (50%)	4 (8%)	5 (10%)	1 (2%)	9 (18%)	6 (12%)	50 (100%)
GENDER							
Male	15 (50%)	4 (13%)	4 (13%)	1 (3%)	4 (13%)	2 (7%)	30 (100%)
Female	10 (50%)	0 (0%)	1 (5%)	0 (0%)	5 (25%)	4 (20%)	20 (100%)
DEGREE							
J.D.	8 (67%)	0 (10%)	2 (17%)	0 (0%)	2 (17%)	0 (0%)	12 (100%)
M.D.	6 (50%)	1 (8%)	1 (8%)	0 (0%)	2 (17%)	2 (17%)	12 (100%)
Ph.D.	11 (42%)	3 (12%)	2 (8%)	1 (4%)	5 (19%)	4 (15%)	26 (100%)

teachers and counselors had played in their lives. There was an interesting gender difference here though, also. While all of the female subjects had been good or excellent students throughout their school careers, and teachers and counselors (with a few exceptions) had been generally supportive of them, few of the women had real mentoring experiences. On the other hand, among the male subjects, though a fair number of them had had uneven academic backgrounds, many more people stepped forward to be their mentors. Typical of the kinds of mentoring experiences these students had were the following:

> I had a substitute teacher who took regular interest in me. . . . She took it upon herself to start showing me around. And on her own she started taking me to different colleges and universities throughout southern California and making appointments with deans and having me talk to them. . . . She exposed me to possibilities I would not have thought of otherwise . . . she also became involved with [my father] and kind of educated him on the need to have me relieved of my family obligations and continue my education.

A sociology professor recalled the person who made all the difference for him:

> Well there's no doubt that the most important person in probably my whole educational experience was a teacher I had in fifth and sixth grade who I visited to tell her I was getting my Ph.D. and that I really owed it to her. She was a wonderful woman, an Anglo woman who was from the Midwest. She was very religious and she had an old-fashioned attitude toward education. She loves her students and she puts out for them. I remember very clearly she bought the World Book Encyclopedia for the class. . . . Up until then I could hardly write my name . . . I could hardly read. She was the kind of person who would take the slowest students and work with them the most. . . . She took me and . . . and she took this one Anglo boy who was a migrant worker . . . he used to wear rags to school. . . . I started doing a lot of book reports and stuff from the World Book Encyclopedia. She introduced me to libraries and to reading and that's when I really started picking up because once I discovered reading it just opened up a whole new world. . . . In those two years I learned how to learn.

One of the minority of female subjects who had had an important mentoring relationship recalled the Anglo history teacher she met in junior college and who she considered to be "the most fantastic woman I have ever met":

> She just really supported me in every way she could . . . she followed me through all the way. In fact, she's the one who got me into UCLA. I never heard of UCLA. She's the one that helped me get the scholarship. She really pushed me. It was like, "You can do it." She

always used to say that she knew I was going to make it big. Where she got it from, I don't know. She kept pushing me and pushing me, and she became a very close friend of our family. Dr. Bailey was also sort of a mentor to . . . a lot of Chicanos who came from East L.A. [Subject mentioned the names of several prominent Chicano males.]

All of the subjects' mentors were not found in school, however. Twenty percent of the subjects cited an older sibling as the person who had been most influential in encouraging their higher education and "showing them the ropes." These were always older sisters and brothers who had had some experience with college themselves. Similarly, it appeared that in the cases where these subjects were the oldest child in the family, either in an absolute sense or the oldest of their gender, they played a mentoring role for their siblings; in 60 percent of these cases, all, or all but one, of the succeeding children also went on to, or were clearly on track for, college.

Fifteen percent of the subjects found mentors outside of the home and school. This was commonly a priest. As a fatherless male subject recounted, the priest had provided the encouragement for him to make the decision to go to college:

At that time, you see, Father Bernardin was already involved in our family. . . . He was a real good man. [In an attempt to model him] I knew that I was going on to further studies and to a monastery. . . . But he never really tried to encourage me [to become a priest]. In fact, I think he thought it would have been a good idea for me to go to college first. Maybe he sensed it.

This subject did later enter the seminary, but exited before becoming a priest, to become a clinical psychologist.

SUMMARY OF SCHOOL AND NEIGHBORHOOD EFFECTS

Most of these subjects attended schools that were very different from the communities in which they resided. Although it is commonly assumed that poor parents are unable to exercise much choice in where their children attend school, this apparently was not the case for many of these academically ambitious students. While it is difficult to judge the extent to which parents may have made housing decisions on the basis of available schools, there is some evidence from other studies of Mexican American housing patterns that upwardly mobile, ambitious families may choose to live in communities that border more prosperous, nonminority areas, which can result in the children attending schools outside the heart of the barrio. Moreover, a substantial percentage of these families opted for Catholic educations for their children, in spite of their very limited incomes. Scholarships and help from other family members made this possible. Finally, the subjects themselves, in collaboration with their siblings, sometimes made the decision to leave their communities and attend schools outside the barrio that they perceived to be academically superior. The result was that more than two-thirds of the subjects attended naturally desegregated or mostly Anglo schools usually in middle- and upper-middle-class neighborhoods, notwithstanding the fact that most lived in low-income and racially isolated neighborhoods.

Curriculum tracking was a powerful force in providing opportunity and shaping aspirations of these subjects. Without the courses they were able to take in the upper track, they would not have been eligible for the college opportunities that they sought. However, tracking operated in complex and even paradoxical ways. For these individuals, all of whom finally, and not always easily, found themselves in the college-bound group, tracking "cocooned" them with high-achieving peers and exposed them to information necessary for getting ahead in the system. For most low-income Chicano students, curriculum tracking serves exactly the opposite function.

Attending desegregated schools provided these subjects not only with a peer group that was savvy about opportunity, but it allowed them to gain the confidence to compete in world class universities. Many subjects commented on how knowing that they could get As while competing with nonminority students sent a powerful signal to them that they could compete and thrive in a college environment.

FIVE

Peers

There is considerable evidence that peers do influence achievement behavior (Epstein & Karweit, 1983; Steinberg et al., 1988). Students whose school friends are high achievers tend to rise to the level of accomplishment of their peers (D'Amico, 1975; Epstein & Karweit, 1983), and students who choose friends who are inclined toward dropping out are at much higher risk for dropping out of school themselves (Rumberger, 1991). However, the relative influence of peers versus parents and others may vary substantially among racial and ethnic groups (Steinberg, Dornbusch, & Brown, 1992). Recent studies have reported finding that parental influence on academic and career decision-making is significantly greater for Hispanic youth than for their non-Hispanic counterparts, thereby reducing the relative power of peers for Latino students (Steinberg, Dornbusch, & Brown, 1992; Clayton et al., 1992). However, as Steinberg, Dornbusch, & Brown (1992) have noted, among Asians and Anglo middle-class groups, where there is likely to be congruence of support for educational goals on the part of both parents and peers, positive academic outcomes are strengthened. Unfortunately, this scenario is less common among African Americans and Hispanics, who are represented disproportionately in the underclass. In fact, high academic achievement has been shown to be a liability in gaining status among peers for many African American and Latino students in inner city schools (Coleman, 1961; Fordham & Ogbu, 1986). For these students, there is the constant threat of alienating their peers by being perceived as "acting white." Hence, they develop and pledge allegiance to an oppositional culture which resists the demands of school. How, then, did this sample of fifty high-achieving Chicano students manage to avoid the potentially negative effects of peer pressure?

Some did not. Not all of these students were uniformly successful throughout school, and some did succumb to negative peer pressure for periods of time. The difference between these students and the typical dropout, however, appears to have been a sense a control over their own circum-

71

stances; the belief that they *could* perform in school if they chose to. Werner and Smith (1989) describe this phenomenon as an "internal locus of control" and cite it as a primary factor in the resiliency demonstrated by some of the children of poverty who they studied.

One subject who was an outstanding student in elementary school talked about how the peer pressure changed between elementary and junior high school in his mostly Chicano, South Texas schools:

> It wasn't vogue to be smart, it wasn't vogue to be number one. And so, you just sort of sat back and [became] your basic C student all through junior high school.
>
> [Interviewer: And high school?]
>
> Same thing. I was very turned off by my high school. I thought the people who made it [in honor society] were a big farce. I didn't want to have anything to do with it. I really felt like I knew my own potential and I really felt like high school was not a place where I need necessarily express it.

Another subject talked about the strategy he used to keep up his grades and still save face with his friends:

> Most of us kids were not studious. Most of us were . . . not too concerned about school. But I always kept it up anyway. I thought it was fun to talk about not studying, but I did it anyway. . . . I didn't let on that I was studying or working hard. I mean you were cool if you didn't study.

Other researchers (for example, Rutter, 1979; Werner & Smith, 1989) have written about the importance of "protective factors" in shielding children from the potentially negative influences of poverty and disadvantage. This literature yields a consensus around three major factors, any one of which may be sufficient to overcome the risk of poor developmental outcomes. These include a positive relationship with at least one caring adult, the communication of high expectations for the child, and opportunities to participate meaningfully in family or group endeavors (Benard, 1991). Every one of these subjects enjoyed at least one of these protective factors as a part of their lives; most could count all three among their arsenal of weapons against poverty and disadvantage. Perhaps this fact helps to explain, as well, the limited and short-term effects of negative peer pressure on those who experienced it.

The vast majority of the subjects, however, effectively managed to avoid negative peer pressure altogether. Most of these subjects, including all of the women, performed well throughout school and did not attempt to hide this fact from their peers. Moreover, few of these subjects reported being "loners" in school and none reported having difficulty maintaining supportive peer relations. In fact, many were social superstars: student-body presidents and the like. Nor did these subjects reject friendships with lower-achieving Chicano peers. Their success in balancing these seemingly contradictory social demands resulted from the structure of their schooling and their own strong sense of cultural identity and self-efficacy.

PEER COMPETITION AND VALIDATION

Inasmuch as nearly 70 percent of the subjects reported that their high schools were composed of mostly Anglos or a broad mix of ethnic groups, and academic tracking further sorted students by ethnic background, with the lower income students of color being placed in the general education track and the high-performing middle-class and Anglo students being placed in the college-prep tracks, the school peer group of most of this sample was white. Being tracked into classes with students who were mostly middle class, white, and who, in the words of one subject, "would have been aghast if they knew that my parents were farmworkers and we lived in labor camps" had consequences for how these subjects came to see themselves. For many, it required that they constantly defend themselves against self-doubt.

Many of the male subjects talked about the importance of competing against middle-class, non-Chicano classmates. (Curiously, this was mentioned frequently by males, but only rarely by females.) Many pegged their own performance against the standard set by particular white, Asian, or Jewish students. They believed that if they were competing favorably against these students, they were probably pretty capable. One subject talked at great length about this phenomenon:

> [T]hrough high school there was always an identified competitor—male or female . . . it was always like neck and neck. Like a racetrack. In high school the competition got really heavy. There were all these Anglo guys, you know, and they were like geniuses . . . there was Ronald, red-haired guy, John, a Jewish guy. Billy, red-haired guy (I never saw red-haired guys in my life before), Steve, big blond guy. All of these were middle-class, you know, they were well-to-do. . . . There were six. . . . And grades would be posted . . . and we would be separated by whiskers: 95.2, 95.4, things like that.

> [Interviewer: And where were you?]

> I was usually at the top.

> [Interviewer: In the top three?]

> The top one. I would trade off with Ron, the red-headed guy.

Some subjects felt the challenge to prove they were capable, not against any specific student but against all the others who were not Chicano:

> To myself, I always had to show the Anglo kids, and the teachers, that just because I was Mexican, I wasn't dumb. When I was in school, I always got top awards. Like I got the only English award, in a school that was mainly Anglo! I thought because I was Mexican that was one thing I could show them, that Mexicans could do better than they could.

Another subject expressed similar attitudes:

> I think the one basic attitude that helped me a lot to do well was a very competitive attitude, especially with the Anglo kids—to be better than them. So I always in my classes loved doing better than them, and I think when I really started coming out was in the ninth grade. I started shining higher than those kids in certain subjects, especially things like social studies.

Occasionally the nonminority peers to whom these subjects were exposed served as important sources of information and actually provided the impetus for subjects to acquire the coursework that would be critical in making the transition to college. One woman recalled the fateful day she went to sign up for high school classes:

> I had to go to school to register and there was this huge line and I was by myself, so I got in line because I found that this was where you got in line if you wanted the general course which was to prepare you just for the basics. The girl in the other line was a girl I had gone to school with, her name was Rema, she said, "Don't get in that line, get in this line; this is for college prep." I told her that was not for me, and she said, "Yes it is," and so I went with her because I didn't want to be alone. . . . When I got in line, she talked me into it by saying, "Don't stand in that line because you will learn the same stuff you learned in seventh and eighth grade, just reviewing the same stuff."

While the college-prep track afforded few opportunities for these subjects to interact with other Latino students, a few subjects maintained a Chicano friendship group at school, and in these cases, the friends, though they often did poorly themselves, tended to be supportive of the subjects' academic achievements. This willingness to be supportive of a friend's academic achievement appeared to be tied to feelings that the achiever was "still on their side" even if he or she performed more like the Anglo kids. One subject who had a crippling case of polio recounted how he was supported by his Chicano peers:

There were a lot of Chicanos in the class, and at the end of the semester, when the teacher read off the grades, all the Chicanos were getting Cs and Ds and Fs, and he got to my name and I got an A. The only Chicano who got an A in the class. And all the Chicanos cheered, "Yayyy!" "Right on." . . . I was different to the extent that I couldn't work out in the fields, and I couldn't get in track, I couldn't wrestle, stuff like that. So what I was doing was getting the grades and excelling scholastically. And rather than making me different and turning everyone off, I was the one they cheered on.

A young woman who used her academic skills to help her friends also found support in her Chicana peer group:

We were about six, seven girls . . . like a clique. But none of them went to college. They got married after high school . . . worked in factories . . . [but] then I was very popular because I helped them with their work and with school. And actually a lot of people say that bright kids were made fun of and all that, but in my case, it wasn't the case. It was the opposite. They would look up . . . and say, "She's so smart," and "She's a brain," and like that. But in a nice way, you know.

Mehan, Hubbard, and Villanueva (1994), in their work with college-bound minority students who have been "detracked" through the AVID (Advancement via Individual Determination) program in San Diego, California schools, have found a similar phenomenon in which high-achieving Chicano students have been successful in avoiding negative stereotyping associated with their academic achievement. According to the authors, these

students seem to have developed an ideology, a consciousness if you will, that is neither oppositional nor conformist. Instead, it combines a belief in achievement with a cultural affirmation, becoming more critical than conformist . . . these students' ideology provides an interesting counterpoint to the ideology of resistance. Here we encounter circumstances in which members of ethnic- and linguistic-minority groups eschew oppositional ideologies in favor of the "accommodation without assimilation" belief system (Gibson, 1988), which is presumably reserved for members of voluntary immigrant groups. (p. 113)

The authors suggest that this ideology is developed, at least in part, through being isolated into special classes that meet on a daily basis. Hence, the ideology developed within this context is supported and reinforced in daily contact with peers who share the same belief system. Exactly how these students are protected from the pressures of a competing peer ideology is not precisely spelled out; however, the authors do suggest that AVID students, like the subjects of this study, negotiated "dual identities" or reference groups.

DUAL REFERENCE GROUPS

A particular phenomenon of multiple reference groups has been noted in recent literature on high academic achievement among socioeconomically disadvantaged groups, and among Hispanics in particular. Gibson (1993) refers to this phenomenon as "additive acculturation" and finds evidence of it in several ethnic groups:

> Recent studies show that many first and second generation immigrant children are successful not because they relinquish their traditional ways but because they draw strength from their home cultures and a positive sense of their ethnic identity. They distinguish the acquisition of school skills and the gaining of proficiency in the ways of the mainstream from their own social identification with a particular ethnic group. (p. 7)

In a study of high-achieving Hispanic students from the High School and Beyond data set, So (1987) noted a similar phenomenon. High achieving Latinos from low-income backgrounds were found to have dual reference groups: they identified with *both* middle-class values and their own ethnic group. In fact, So found that while the middle-class reference group had a greater effect on educational achievement than the Hispanic reference group (once again demonstrating the relatively weak negative effects of low-performing peers), "those who aspire to the middle class, as well as maintain strong communicative skills within the Hispanic culture, outperform those who do not aspire to the middle class and do not maintain strong communicative skills with their parents and reference group. . . . [A] high achieving disadvantaged student can retain minority group identity while at the same time aspiring to membership in the middle class" (pp. 30–31).

Consistent with these findings, most of these subjects maintained two peer groups: one at school and one from their neighborhood. Because they were so segregated by classes at school, it was easy to keep the two separate. At school, they were free to compete academically in the classroom, and when they went home in the afternoon they would assume a very different posture. This subject, a high-level federal policymaker, described the two social worlds in which he lived:

> In high school . . . I got involved in all the clubs. I was an officer. I got scholarships, I was in all the college prep classes. I was getting As and Bs. I was associating with the white kids, but only on a superficial level, as in those clubs. Once out of school, I became a

rowdy, a *pachuco* like the rest. By that time I was riding around in cars, drinking and stealing and skipping out of restaurants. All that kind of stupid thing.

Others, like the Harvard-educated community organizer, found peer groups that had different orientations, but were not quite so disparate:

> I hung out in high school with smart, good kids . . . studious, mostly girls, white girls. . . . The smart ones, you know, were active and ran the clubs and I was part of that. . . . So I had two sets of friends, Mexican friends and my white friends. Outside of school . . . [we] formed our own band. All-Mexican band.

Because the phenomenon of maintaining multiple peer groups was so pervasive, by the time they had graduated from high school, these subjects had had excellent training in moving between two cultures. They knew how to handle themselves with high achieving Anglos, and they were still equally comfortable in the company of friends who would never leave the fields, the barrios, or go to college. For the most part, they were able to make the jump into the mainstream, without alienating the communities from which they came. It is easy to see how this social adaptability could become a great advantage later in life, and a major factor in their continued academic success.

SIX

Personal Attributes and Individual Differences

LANGUAGE

For Latinos, language has long been thought to be the chief barrier to educational and occupational advancement. Much of the discussion surrounding the early development of bilingual education programs for Latino students in the United States centered around the idea that if Spanish-speaking children could be taught English when they arrived at school, their educational problems would essentially be solved (Cummins, 1981). Of course, this turned out to be an overly simplistic analysis of the educational problems of Latino students. Nonetheless, early efforts at bilingual education programs focused on "transitioning" students as quickly as possible into English. In order to accomplish this aim, Latino parents often were counseled to speak only English at home, thereby providing "good" language models for their children. The difficult process of shifting from the native language of the parents to the use of English within the family is recounted movingly in the following passage from *Hunger of Memory* by Richard Rodriguez (1982).

> [O]ne Saturday morning three nuns arrived at the house to talk with our parents. . . . I overheard one voice gently wondering, "Do your children only speak Spanish at home, Mrs. Rodriguez?" . . . "Is it possible for you and your husband to encourage your children to practice their English when they are at home?" . . . Again and again in the days following, increasingly angry, I was obliged to hear my mother and father: "Speak to us *en ingles.*" But the special feeling of closeness at home was diminished by then. . . . Matching the silence I started hearing in public was a new quiet at home. The family's quiet

was partly due to the fact that, as we children learned more and more English, we shared fewer and fewer words with our parents. . . . After English became my primary language, I no longer knew what words to use in addressing my parents. The old Spanish words (those tender accents of sound) I had used earlier—*mama* and *papa*—I couldn't use anymore. They would have been too painful reminders of how much had changed in my life. . . . My mother . . . grew restless, seemed troubled and anxious at the scarcity of words exchanged in the house . . . [My father] seemed reconciled to the new quiet . . . he retired into silence. At dinner he spoke very little. (pp. 20–24)

The objective of this strategy was to convert Spanish-speaking students into monolingual English speakers, inasmuch as "bilingualism," or the use of two languages, was seen as a major impediment to academic achievement. In fact, a number of studies have documented the relationship between use of Spanish in the home and lower achievement scores of Latino students (Darcy, 1953; Durán, Enright, & Rock, 1985). However, this research often suffered from methodological flaws.

More recent research has dispelled the myth that bilingualism, or the use of Spanish in the home, is the source of Latino underachievement (Cummins, 1981; Durán, Enright, & Rock, 1985). However the popular perception that the primary goal of bilingual education should be to transition students into English—and out of their primary language—as quickly as possible remains deeply imbedded in educational practice in American schools. What insight might the language characteristics of this sample of high-achieving Chicanos yield for our understanding of the role of language in achievement?

If, indeed, the use of English in the home holds an academic advantage for Chicano students, then we would expect to find that the majority of the sample came from English-speaking homes. This was not the case (see table 6.1). Of the total sample, only 8 subjects, or 16 percent, had come from homes in which English was the primary language. The largest percentage of subjects spoke only Spanish at home, and two-thirds began school without knowing English. But there are clues in how they describe both language and literacy in the home that illuminate the role of what Cummins (1981) has called "additive bilingualism" in their academic development. Unlike students who are rapidly transitioned out of their first language into a second, additive bilinguals use the firm foundation in the first language to build linguistically and cognitively in both languages. Thus, their cognitive skills are enhanced by capitalizing on the reservoir of proficiencies already developed in the first language. A Chicana professor of political science explained how her parents, monolingual Spanish speakers, with only first- and third-grade formal educations, nurtured literacy and a love of reading in their home:

Table 6.1. *Subjects' Home Language*

	English	Spanish	Bilingual	Total
TOTAL	8 (16%)	25 (50%)	17 (34%)	50 (100%)
GENDER				
Males	4 (13%)	13 (43%)	13 (40%)	30 (100%)
Females	4 (20%)	12 (60%)	4 (20%)	20 (100%)
DEGREE				
J. D.	1 (8%)	8 (67%)	3 (25%)	12 (100%)
M.D.	3 (25%)	5 (42%)	4 (33%)	12 (100%)
Ph. D.	4 (15%)	12 (46%)	10 (38%)	26 (100%)

[W]hen we were little kids my mother was always the person who had to help us when we had to learn things and memorize, recite things. . . . [M]y father used to conduct classes [for the older siblings] and teach them how to read and write Spanish, and things about Mexico, and a lot of history . . . that's why I am saying that there was a lot of help in the sense of—we were very poor—but there were always [Spanish] magazines in the house, books in the house, and newspapers in the house. My mother always had that . . . she may not have had money to buy a dress or something, but we always had those things.

While few of the subjects used English at home with their parents, almost two-thirds of the subjects engaged in important literacy activities—discussing current events and political issues—with their parents and siblings as they grew up. This kind of activity is illustrative of the point made by Cummins (1981), when he stated that "whether English or a minority language is used in the home is, in itself, relatively unimportant for students' academic development . . . what is important for future academic success is the quality of interaction children experience with adults" (p. 41).

PERSONAL CHARACTERISTICS

When asked what personal characteristic made it possible for these fifty to realize their high academic aspirations, subjects cited a number of specific factors. Among the lengthy list of responses were fear of failure, ambition, curiosity, good memory, and knowing how to get things done. Most of these characteristics, however, were highly individualistic and were seldom cited by more than one or two other people. "Knowing what I wanted" (goal direction) and "self-discipline" were each mentioned by a little more than 10 percent of the subjects. Many people, more than one quarter, also credited themselves with being hardworkers. Recalling the subjects' descriptions of their parents as

Table 6.2. *Personal Characteristics Most Critical to Academic Attainment**

	Persistence	Hardwork	Ability	Social Skill	Self Discipline	Goal Orientation
TOTAL	25 (50%)	13 (26%)	11 (22%)	8 (16%)	6 (12%)	6 (12%)
GENDER						
Male	15 (50%)	10 (30%)	6 (20%)	7 (23%)	4 (13%)	2 (7%)
Female	10 (50%)	3 (15%)	5 (25%)	1 (5%)	2 (10%)	4 (20%)
DEGRE						
J.D.	7 (58%)	5 (42%)	3 (25%)	2 (17%)	1 (8%)	1 (8%)
M.D.	6 (50%)	4 (33%)	3 (25%)	2 (17%)	0 (0%)	3 (25%)
Ph.D.	12 (46%)	4 (15%)	5 (19%)	4 (15%)	5 (19%)	2 (8%)

* Table lists all characteristics that were mentioned by more than 10 percent of sample; rows do not sum to 100 percent because most subjects named more than one characteristic.

"the hardest workers I've ever known," it was not surprising to find that so many subjects would value this quality and find it in themselves. Given the central importance placed upon ability and intelligence in the academy, however, it *was* surprising that fewer than one-fourth of the subjects mentioned ability or intelligence as a characteristic they considered key to their academic success.

The single characteristic that was most salient to these subjects, and cited by more than half as key, was persistence. This was described using terms such as "tenacious," "stubborn," "persevering," but most often simply "persistent" (see table 6.2).

Ability versus Effort

There is a temptation to conclude that false modesty may have lead the subjects to reject "native ability" as the primary factor in their academic accomplishments. Conventional wisdom suggests that people who excel academically are simply more intelligent than those who do not. However, there is considerable evidence that intellectual ability (as measured by standardized tests) and academic attainment are not necessarily highly correlated, especially among minorities (Durán, 1983). And there is some support for the idea that persistence may play a larger role in many intellectual and academic endeavors than would seem apparent. Simonton (1987), in his review of achieved eminence, found that persistence was more powerful than ability by itself in explaining the prodigious accomplishments of a sample of outstanding achievers. Cox (1926, in Simonton, 1987), commenting on a study of highly talented individuals, noted "that high but not the highest intelligence, combined with the greatest degree of persistence, will achieve greater eminence than the highest degree of intelligence with somewhat less persistence" (p. 138).

One subject, a psychologist, offered the following comment on the role of intelligence versus hard work in his own academic career:

I knew I wasn't all that smart. I knew that [if] I hadn't studied, it just [wouldn't] come like that. I had to study for my mind to work. . . . There were people with more smarts. When people, for example, say to me, "Oh yeah, you're a real brain, aren't you," I say, "I'm not a brain." I knew I wasn't. I was not a genius. I knew that. All I could do was study hard, that's all. . . . But I'd always get a good feeling from mastering something. And that's a personal characteristic. I would get a good feeling from coming out on top of the heap of people who took the test. It was real, it just was. It was my own internal reward.

Another subject commented on how drive rather than native ability was responsible not only for his academic acumen but for success in other endeavors as well:

I think that people admired the fact that I worked hard. I think people admired the fact that I was an achiever when I really shouldn't have been. People would look at me and think to themselves, "There is no reason why this guy should be as good as he is in everything." Academically, the counselors would look at me and say, "This guy has an IQ of 95; there is no reason he should be doing this well." And then I would work hard and I would get As and I would impress them. . . . The coaches would look at me and say, "Hey, this guy weighs 90 pounds—are you kidding?—if you go out on the field, you'll get blown away." I would go out there and I would become the number one, you know, the starting man on the track team, and they would admire me. So that's a quality—maybe stubbornness more than anything else.

One subject, a lawyer and corporate executive, seemed to sum up best what many others felt. Clearly, a certain amount of intellectual ability was a prerequisite to academic success, but in his case, as in many others, that ability, which was not perceived to be extraordinary, was just sufficient to allow other, more salient qualities to develop:

Well, in terms of sheer intellectual ability, I think that maybe I am in the top ten percent, which, with the people I see myself competing with . . . it's not overwhelming . . . it's not overwhelming at Stanford; it's not overwhelming in terms of the national leadership, but that gives me enough that I can bring into play things that I think a lot of the 10 percent do not have, which is, number one, a sense of purpose beyond the person, which is a great motivator. Because when you run out of motivation for yourself, and you don't have anything else, you just can't go that extra mile.

The social-cognitive perspective as articulated by Bandura (1990) suggests that such persistence is, in fact, the result of a "self-belief of efficacy" which, consistent with the sugjects' interpretations, is quite different from ability or intelligence. This belief in one's own efficacy is engendered by experiences of mastery, modeling the behavior of important others, and being the recipeint of social persuasion, that is, having been told by others that they are capable. As recounted by the subjects, all of these experiences were factors in their own development. It is this self-belief of efficacy, according to Bandura, which determines how much effort a person will exert in an endeavor, and how long they will persevere in the face of obstacles. Hence a "striking characteristic of people who have achieved eminence in their fields is an inextinguishable sense of efficacy and a firm belief in the worth of what they are doing. This resilient self-belief system enable[s] them to override repeated early rejections . . ." (p. 317)

Certainly some reasonable level of ability was a prerequisite to their academic success, and most subjects acknowledge this, but there was widespread agreement that ability alone would not have made their educational journeys possible. Persistence and hard work were the sine qua non of educational mobility, and perhaps, as one academic put it, compliance:

I think those of us who made it through are not the most intelligent. The most intelligent are probably the ones who dropped out. We're the ones who were the most compliant.

Social Isolation

More than a third of the subjects described themselves as skinny, small, or late-maturing during their secondary school years. These characteristics were perceived to have excluded them from many of the activities that they saw fellow students engaging in, and to some extent to have isolated them from peers. One subject commented on how he "didn't join a gang, because, being small, I didn't think I would survive." Others talked about how they didn't pursue sports and other activities which would have taken time away from studies because of their size or lack of physical maturity. Another ten subjects (20 percent) commented on how physical illness was also a factor in their relations with peers. A physician, one of six subjects who was asthmatic as a child, described how this fact helped to keep him under the strict control of his parents:

> As a result of my asthma I was very sheltered. I could only be out
> before it got too cold. Because at night is when the asthma attacks,
> so I could only stay out until about six p.m.

A professor of education recounted how her illness had isolated her from
peers at a critical time in her development:

> Around puberty it really got out of hand. . . . I was in a wheelchair
> and I had difficulty getting around so I was home-taught, therefore
> not allowing me to have social interactions with kids my age. I
> became out of touch.

Another subject spent one of his high school years in a hospital being treated
for tuberculosis, and yet another suffered the crippling effects of polio. For a
substantial portion of the subjects, size and ill health may have had an impact
in channeling their energies into schoolwork, and away from other competing
endeavors.

Phenotype

For any racial or ethnic minority group a certain advantage can accrue to the
ability to "pass," that is, to physically blend in with the dominant culture. There
is a substantial literature on the links between economic opportunity and skin
color in African Americans, concluding that darker-skinned Blacks experience
more discrimination and less occupational mobility than lighter-skinned
Blacks (Arce, Murguia, & Frisbie, 1987). Additionally, several researchers have
found that European features and lighter skin color enhance life chances and
earnings for Mexican Americans as well. In a sample of nearly one thousand
Mexican American males, lighter skinned, European-looking Chicanos were
found to have completed more years of education, to hold higher status
positions, and to earn significantly more money than did their darker-skinned,
more Indian-featured brethren (Arce, Murguia, & Frisbie, 1987; Telles &
Murguia, 1990). Moreover, Bloom (1991) noted that light skin color was also
an advantage to Mexican American children in the way they were evaluated
by their teachers in bilingual classrooms. While the Bloom study did not
incorporate an index of European versus Mexican facial features, she found
that teachers were more apt to judge Mexican American students with light
skin color as academically capable than they were their darker-skinned peers.
These findings beckon the question: Were the study subjects somehow
advantaged by their physical appearance?

Few of the subjects (16 percent) were dark skinned, and 60 percent were
judged to be either European looking or to have an ambiguous appearance
which could be taken for a Mediterranean background. Nonetheless, when
asked if they felt they looked "typically Mexican," 82 percent of the sample

said yes. However, most of the subjects did admit to having been mistaken by others for being Greek, Italian, Persian, or some other Southern European ethnic group. When asked if their appearance was, in any way, a factor in their academic achievement, most subjects responded either that it had not been or, in a few cases, that their general attractiveness or unattractiveness had played a role in opportunity. For the most part, subjects did not relate the question about their appearance to the degree to which they looked typically Mexican American. Perhaps this stemmed from their strong sense of kinship with other Chicanos of whatever color, or possibly many had not been aware of the ways in which their particular appearance may have made a difference in the opportunities they encountered. However, one subject with a Ph.D. in education was quite clear about how her light skin had worked to her advantage as she was going through school:

> I was somewhat light-skinned and I was growing up in a Chicano barrio, and with African Americans. I think the teachers thought of me as the next best thing. I knew I was teacher's pet. . . . I remember knowing that teachers had a real distaste for some of the other students . . . everyone else was being treated pretty shabbily. . . . Later in high school when I encountered more white students, by that time it was too late; I already felt pretty good about myself.

An economist who had given some thought to the issue of phenotype and life chances, and who admitted to being called a "*gabacha*" (Anglo) by peers who noted she was not easily identifiable as a Chicana, had an interesting economic theory on the role of phenotype in academic achievement:

> [T]here is a thought among Mexican Americans that the fair-skinned are more likely to assimilate, to make it. So, it could be the reverse; it could be that teachers are more willing to devote their resources to people who might be able to make it in a sense of association.

It is difficult to conclude from the comments of the subjects, to what extent their appearance was a factor in their educational mobility, since most were reluctant to make these linkages. However, the fact that most of subjects were, at most, ambiguous in appearance is consistent with others' findings that phenotype is related to opportunity structure and discrimination in the United States.

FORMULATING EDUCATIONAL GOALS

How and when did these subjects first really decide they were going on to college? Table 6.3 displays the distribution of responses to this question. What is important to note about these data is that there are almost equal numbers of

Table 6.3. *When Subjects Decided to Go to College*

	Prior to Junior High	Junior High	Early High School	Late High School	Later	Total *N*
TOTAL	16 (32%)	8 (16%)	10 (20%)	11 (22%)	5 (10%)	50 (100%)
GENDER						
Male	7 (23%)	5 (17%)	7 (27%)	7 (20%)	4 (13%)	30 (100%)
Female	9 (45%)	3 (15%)	3 (15%)	4 (20%)	1 (5%)	20 (100%)
DEGREE						
J.D.	6 (50%)	2 (17%)	3 (25%)	0 (0%)	1 (8%)	12 (100%)
M.D.	2 (17%)	2 (17%)	5 (42%)	3 (25%)	0 (0%)	12 (100%)
Ph.D.	8 (31%)	4 (15%)	2 (8%)	8 (31%)	4 (15%)	26 (100%)

individuals who decided very early and who did not decide until late in high school (generally senior year), or even sometime after having graduated from high school, that they would go to college.

Who decided early and who decided late? Women tended to decide to go to college earlier than their male peers; as a group they were always more academically-oriented than the males. Students who went on to get the Ph.D., on the other hand, were much more likely than the others to make a late college decision. Likewise, this group was also more likely to decide to continue their education to the doctoral level after having entered college and completing an undergraduate degree. This may be explained by the fact that the parents of these subjects had a limited knowledge of professional careers. They were familiar with doctors, lawyers, and pharmacists and encouraged their children's aspirations along these lines. Hence, these academically ambitious students who set their sites early on a college education often did so with the idea in mind that they would become a doctor, lawyer, or pharmacist. (Several of the subjects found their way into medicine through an early interest in pharmacy.) Perhaps not surprisingly, none of the subjects had been encouraged to pursue an academic career or become a professor. Parents had no contact with, or knowledge of, this kind of career. This aspiration was realized once the subject already had experience in the world of academia. Working class academics are the products of their peer associations and the encouragement of professors within the university (Ryan & Sackrey, 1984).

Tables 6.4 and 6.5 display information on the academic performance of study subjects up to the point of entering college. Table 6.4 shows the responses to the question "Did you ever do especially poorly in school (C grades and below)?" In all cases, individuals who had done poorly early in their school careers attributed this to difficulty with the English language. Two-thirds of the sample spoke only Spanish or a combination of English and Spanish when they began school. The women, in particular, however, made a rapid transition to English and quickly began performing well in school, which

Table 6.4. *Whether Subjects Ever Did Poorly in School Prior to College (Cs or less)*

	Yes	No	Total *N*
TOTAL	24 (48%)	26 (52%)	50 (100%)
GENDER			
Male	20 (67%)	10 (33%)	30 (100%)
Female	4 (20%)	16 (80%)	20 (100%)
DEGREE			
J.D.	5 (42%)	7 (58%)	12 (100%)
M.D.	6 (50%)	6 (50%)	12 (100%)
Ph.D.	13 (50%)	13 (50%)	26 (100%)

Table 6.5. *When Subjects Began to Get Good Grades (Bs or better)*

	Always/ Throughout	Elementary	Junior High	High School	Never Prior To College	Total *N*
TOTAL	36 (73%)	8 (16%)	1 (2%)	4 (8%)	1 (2%)	50 (100%)
GENDER						
Male	16 (53%)	8 (27%)	1 (3%)	4 (13%)	1 (3%)	30 (100%)
Female	20 (100%)	0 (0%)	0 (0%)	0 (0%)	0 (0%)	20 (100%)
DEGREE						
J.D.	10 (83%)	1 (8%)	0 (0%)	1 (8%)	0 (0%)	12 (100%)
M.D.	9 (75%)	2 (17%)	0 (0%)	1 (8%)	0 (0%)	12 (100%)
Ph.D.	17 (65%)	5 (19%)	1 (4%)	2 (8%)	1 (4%)	26 (100%)

explains the apparent discrepancy with table 6.5, in which all of the women report that they had always been good students.

The most important feature of tables 6.4 and 6.5 is the fact that five of the subjects, all males, reported that they had not even begun to perform well in school until sometime in high school or later, and almost two-thirds reported having a period in school in which they did not do well. Unlike the females, several male subjects began their elementary school careers performing well, and later, for a variety of reasons, sometimes because of peer pressure, performed poorly in school. In sum, the school careers of these exceptionally high achieving Chicano (male) students often displayed an uneven performance. At different points in their precollegiate education they undoubtedly looked very much like other Chicano students who do not go on to college.

SUMMARY OF PERSONAL ATTRIBUTES

A number of personal traits and dispositions characterized the subjects of this study in ways that clearly had an impact on their educational ambitions.

Although a multitude of studies have correlated use of English with increased academic achievement, these individuals came overwhelmingly from homes where Spanish was the primary language. But because literacy was valued in their homes, they became "additive bilinguals": individuals who build a second language onto the firm foundation of a first, so that they continue to develop linguistically and cognitively in both languages. For most, the advantage of having skills in two languages continued to pay dividends in their chosen professions. Most of the professionals counted Spanish-speaking clients as an important percentage of their client base, and many academics used their facility with Spanish language and culture in their research.

With respect to personality characteristics, the subjects described themselves as persistent and not the most intellectually capable of their ethnic peers. They felt that drive and motivation were more critical factors in realizing their own ambitions than native talent.

Nearly half of the study subjects characterized themselves as excessively small, weak, or puny (this is a male issue much more than a female one) or as having a physical condition that isolated them from peers. Size was an issue more for the males as it prevented them from participating in athletics and other activities that could have taken time away from academic pursuits. Physical handicaps were instrumental in a number of cases in channeling the subjects' energies into reading when they were unable to socialize with peers.

By a large margin, these subjects were either light-skinned and/or European-looking, or their physical appearance was ambiguous. Few of the sample looked "classically Mexican" in both skin color and features. Studies of phenotype and economic opportunity, conducted largely on African Americans, have shown that the ability to "pass" in American society can substantially enhance life chances and economic mobility.

Finally, there were substantial differences in the academic performance of males and females. Females, in this sample, were consistently good students and tended to aspire to college early in their school careers. Males demonstrated a more uneven picture of academic development, sometimes delaying the decision to go on to college until after they had completed high school. Many of the males did not appear to be headed for an elite education, even late in their high school years.

This was not the only way in which the male subjects differed from the females. Because their paths to higher education were distinctive in so many ways, the following chapter devotes itself to describing the women in the sample and their particular experiences in climbing over the ivy walls.

SEVEN

The Women

L ittle is known about the educational mobility of women, and even less about minority women's mobility (Holland & Eisenhart, 1990). Until recently, the educational career paths of women were not considered an important topic of research, and most studies, both quantitative and qualitative, focused on male subjects. A notable exception to this is the work of Holland and Eisenhart (1990), in which they studied the experiences of twenty-three women, both African American and white, through their undergraduate years at two Southern universities. The women had been selected, in particular, because they had demonstrated a unique potential: they were all headed for careers in science. What Holland and Eisenhart discovered over the years they spent with these young women was both troubling and instructive; although the women no doubt began their college careers with somewhat different expectations, rather than supporting women's educational aspirations, "at both [universities], the peer culture established an ethos for women that emphasized romantic relationships with men as a major route to self-worth and prestige" (p. 118). What the authors witnessed was the gradual decline in aspirations and eventual coming to terms with reduced ambitions for almost all of the women in the study.

The process by which this downward scaling of ambitions occurred was perhaps the most troublesome aspect of the phenomenon. As Holland and Eisenhart note: "In the United States, race, class, and age hierarchies, as they are reflected in the schools, are mediated largely by school authorities. Gender hierarchies, as they are reflected in schools, are mediated largely by peers" . . . campus peer society and culture was the major purveyor of male privilege. From this standpoint, the peer culture emerges as one of the major sites of reproduction of the patriarchal gender hierarchy" (p. 222). Hence, there is no institution against which to resist; the "enemy" of these women's ambitions are their "peers who may sleep in the same room and even in the same bed" (p. 221). In sum, the women, influenced by a peer culture that placed a high premium on romantic relationships and marriage, opted for romance over education.

Holland and Eisenhart's study illuminates the central, yet missing, element in the analysis of educational mobility for Chicanas in this study. By grouping both males and females together, we gain a broader picture of the similarities of experience of both genders, and this is important particularly in analyzing the stereotypes about Mexican family culture. However, these low-income Chicanas were simultaneously dealing with the issues of social-class reproduction and racial/ethnic discrimination while also being confronted with a peer culture that values women in the role of "girlfriend," "wife," and "mother," to such an extent that there is high social risk involved in displacing these roles with those of "lawyer," "physician," or "professor." The central issue for these Chicanas was the circumnavigation of a course that would allow them to pursue their educational goals without alienating themselves from all forms of social and psychological support.

WOMEN OF THE FIRST GENERATION

The twenty women in this study, whose mean age is now forty-eight years, completed their graduate educations roughly a decade and a half ago, during a period in which there was considerable attention paid to issues of equality of opportunity and an emerging consciousness of women's expanding roles in society. Nonetheless, only a handful of Ph.D.'s, M.D.'s, and J.D.'s were awarded to Latinas in the late 1970s. For example, Hispanic women accounted for only .006 percent of all doctoral degrees awarded in 1979, although Latinos comprised approximately eight percent of the population at that time (Carter & Wilson, 1991).

These women were raised in the postwar period, during which most mothers defined themselves as housewives and few role models existed for women outside of the home. Certainly it was rare to encounter a Latina lawyer, physician, or university professor. And then, as now, Anglo Americans (as well as many Chicanos) held very stereotypical views of Mexican American family life and roles (Carter & Segura, 1979). However, opportunity was opening up in the form of minority recruitment, grants, and federally guaranteed loans to attend universities and graduate schools. These subjects are among the first few Mexican American women from low-income backgrounds to take advantage of these opportunities and complete doctoral and professional educations.

One overriding theme that emerges from the stories of these women is that they had followed a very narrow path to their academic accomplishments. They were raised in strict, authoritarian homes where few opportunities were provided to socialize outside of school. Most commented that they were not allowed to date until very late in high school, and even this was controlled by strict curfews. All had been good or outstanding students throughout their precollege years. In fact, as students they were superior to the men. A few had experienced some difficulty in adjusting to the all-English environment of the schools when they began, but all of these women quickly assessed the requirements of the classroom, and by second grade they were already outperforming most of their peers. School was a rewarding place where they acted out the hard work ethic of their largely immigrant parents. But school was much more than a place to achieve; here they were introduced to new ideas through books. Over and over, the women recounted how they found out about the possibilities in the larger world through books. An attorney working in civil rights law talked about the importance of books for her:

> I was very studious because I wanted to read and get a lot of things
> that I couldn't learn in school, but in school I could pick up things
> real easy.

A political science professor summed up her experience with school and learning in the following way:

> I really, really love school. I loved it when I was a little kid and I like it
> now. I don't know why, except maybe that my mother and father always
> emphasized just knowledge for the sake of knowledge and not for the sake of
> achievement. They never asked me about my grades, just, you know, What
> did I really know? What could I do? [T]hey taught me how to read and write in
> Spanish . . . and I didn't get a grade [in that].

In spite of the fact that they were such outstanding students, however, the women cited much less encouragement from people outside of the family than did the men. Women were also less likely to have mentors than their male counterparts. Sixty percent of the males cited a teacher or some other adult outside of the family as having had a major impact on setting their educational goals in their precollege years; only 30 percent of the females reported having had such an experience.

Although all of these women had excellent academic records throughout school (rarely receiving a grade lower than B), four (20 percent) of them had been placed into a noncollege preparatory track at some time during high school. This is compared to the 37 percent of men who had a similar experience. In each case, the woman had to fight her way out of this track, either by arguing with counselors or signing herself up for classes she was not slated to take. By high school's end, all of the women in the sample had been in a college prep track and this became critically important, not only in providing them with the requisite courses to enter the university but also because of the peers to whom they were exposed.

Even more than the men in the sample, most of the women (75 percent) had attended highly mixed or mostly white schools. This resulted in heavy contact with Anglo students, either because there were few non-Anglo students in the school or because they had been tracked into classes where very few other Latino students were placed. These opportunities to interact with the majority culture and test their abilities against what they considered to be an objective standard were reported by the women to be important in gaining the confidence to compete outside that arena. Still, these women maintained social contact and personal bonds with Chicano cousins and peers in their predominantly Mexican American neighborhoods. Many attributed this bicultural experience to the ease they later felt in moving between two cultures.

Virtually every woman could recall teachers who had been encouraging and who were instrumental in raising their self confidence. This was in stark contrast to the many stories of counselors who had either failed to recognize their potential or who stood in their way. Nonetheless, the encouragement the women received from teachers was not generally followed up with advice or counsel on *how* they might realize their educational aspirations in college. Teachers did not usually see themselves in the role of mentors to these women.

Although the women did not find many mentors outside of the home, they usually received considerable support from their families. On the whole, parents encouraged sons and daughters similarly, but they were more specific with their sons about the kinds of roles to which they might aspire. For example, men were more often directed toward a particular career goal, whereas women were simply encouraged in the abstract to do well "so you don't have to depend on anyone." For both men and women, mothers were most often cited as the parent who had the greatest influence on shaping their educational goals. Fathers alone were seldom seen as having played this role.

This was somewhat surprising, though perhaps it should not have been. The initial hypothesis had been that fathers would play a much more pivotal role in their daughter's aspirations, inasmuch as they represented the link to the outside world and would probably have greater access to information about educational and occupational opportunities. However, what was unforeseen was the extent to which the majority of mothers were also working outside of the home and held powerful roles within the family. Hence, while they could not serve as occupational role models for their daughters, the women found much to emulate in their mothers' strong personalities and belief in the future.

Research on intergenerational mobility of women suggests that the mother's occupational status is of primary importance in predicting women's occupations. In fact, the effect of the mother's occupation is of greater relative importance than that of the father in predicting a daughter's occupational inheritance, and this appears to hold, regardless of race, in studies of blacks and whites (Rosenfeld, 1978). Perhaps it is not reaching too far to suggest that the mother's general status in the family might also predict a daughter's upward mobility in the context of low-income homes.

Importantly, these women had not been sidetracked by heterosexual relationships and familial responsibilities. At an age when most Latinas had married and begun to have children, these women remained single. Only one of these women had married prior to graduate school. None had children until her education was nearly complete. How had they protected themselves from such a pervasive cultural imperative? Throughout adolescence and into the transition to college, virtually every one of the women cited an aspect of their lives that set them apart from their age peers and allowed them to accept themselves as "different." For some it was a special talent, like playing the harp, that took all their discretionary time; for others it was an illness that separated them from their peers; still others cited exceptional home responsibilities because of large numbers of siblings, or a physical attribute such as being "fat," that excluded them from peer activities. One woman described how the years she spent in a convent strengthened her resolve to realize her educational ambitions:

> In a convent you are really career-oriented. You really are. And when you come out you really have to get yourself involved. I couldn't see getting involved in all that social stuff because I didn't have the time to do that, going to all the dances, and bars. . . . I couldn't see that for myself because I am very cause oriented and the convent does that to you, and that is what you do with your time.

In addition to these particular experiences, almost all were cloistered within their families by parents who closely monitored their daughter's time away from school. Reading, more than any other single activity, became a central involvement in their lives.

Perhaps the fact that they were not easily averted from their goals was a response to the challenge many of the women felt from extended family members who doubted the wisdom of supporting a daughter's aspirations. A professor of literature cited what many of the women recounted as a common refrain: "My grandmother and my mother's brother . . . they said, why do you send her to school? She's only going to get married." But their educational focus no doubt also resulted from explicit messages from mothers, many of whom had felt their own ambitions thwarted by unfortunate events in their childhoods or unhappy marriages, to "not have to depend on a man." A professor of social work responded to the question, "What was your mother's idea of 'being successful'?", in this way:

> Her idea of being successful in life is to be totally independent of a male in life and she would hope I would fulfill all her dreams, which are to remain single, to be financially independent, and to have a profession.

Holland and Eisenhart (1990), in their investigation of the role of heterosexual relationships in the career choices of both white women and women of
color, concluded that, contrary to popular lore, women who downscale their
ambitions do not curtail their educational aspirations because "they fall in
love"; rather, they fall in love because they have already decided to reduce
their academic goals. By corollary, the women who achieve high levels of
academic success are not the unfortunate few who could not attract a mate,
but are those who have chosen to put their educations and careers first. There
was strong evidence for this position in the first generation sample. For
example, 60 percent of the women, a higher percentage than the men (40
percent), reported having decided they would go to college long before
entering high school, though this may have been conceptualized as attending
the community college nearby. For them, this was not a last-minute decision to
take advantage of an opportunity that presented itself, but more often a life-
long ambition to pursue a higher education. This early college orientation was
also cited as important in helping them to forestall marriage and family
obligations. A biology professor talked about the importance of this decision
for her own career path:

> I was aware of what I didn't want to do. I did not want to get
> married. I did not want to work at the five and dime. . . . I did not see
> that as fulfilling my life and, in fact, I saw it as a way of never getting
> beyond. If I had married right after high school, forget it!

For the women who did marry before completing the doctoral degree,
the marriage partner was invariably also engaged in academic or professional
pursuits and fully supported the woman's ambitions. In this way, marriage
served to reinforce her goals, rather than compete with them. As one psychologist conveyed when asked about especially significant events in her life:

> Meeting my husband, it was essential because I only had my
> bachelor's degree when I met him. He is very gifted, and sort of like
> a very supportive person . . . he thinks people shouldn't waste their
> gifts . . . and both of us don't want any children . . . and both of us
> just want to live life the way we want to . . . and he is very supportive
> of my gifts.

In spite of the fact that these women had completed high school and
continued through college with excellent records that would have qualified
them for scholarships and fellowships, half commented that special recruitment programs were largely responsible for their college and career choices.
Recruitment programs were sources of both information and financial aid that
they had lacked. Most felt that they would not have been able to complete

their educations without special financial aid programs, even in a time when college fees and tuition were much lower, and many would have chosen a much more modest education than the one they ended up completing. A professor of education, one of the few women who made a late decision to attend college, described the way in which recruitment had changed her life course:

> I didn't know what college was up until that point. I was just going to get married. [But] I was given a partial scholarship to X college. I was in the top ten of the graduating class and they selected those students if they had enough units to take one class and to go to college and kind of try it out. So they called me in and said, "Do you want to take this?" I said, "Sure." . . . That was my first exposure to it . . . . I found out that I liked it . . . and so when they said they were offering scholarships to the university, I said, "Sure, I will apply."

The profile that emerges of these academically ambitious Chicanas is one of a carefully screened individual. She had to have been a consistently good student who usually set her goals early and relied on few people outside the family for advice or assistance. At an age when friends were marrying and establishing families, she had remained single and dedicated to her education, eschewing the culture of romance. If she did marry before completing her education, it was generally to a man who shared her educational goals and supported her in attaining them. She had culturally challenging experiences in integrated schools that built the skills and self-confidence to venture into the higher education arena. There was little margin for error; once on the path to higher education, these women did not deviate from that course.

Finally, it is interesting to note that in spite of the self-discipline and reliance on inner resources evidenced by the stories of these women, there was an additional difference between them and their male counterparts. When asked to what they attributed their academic successes, women were more likely to cite something outside of themselves (50 percent versus 27 percent of the males), such as the support of their families, while men more commonly noted a personal characteristic, such as persistence or self-discipline (53 percent versus 35 percent for the females). The tendency for the women to cite factors outside of their own control as responsible for their academic achievements is described in the psychological literature as having an *external locus of control* (Weiner, 1980). Such an orientation is commonly associated with lower achievement motivation, as students do not believe that they can truly affect their own academic fate. However, these findings have been based primarily on studies of white middle class students. The percentages of these very highly motivated Chicanas call into question the extent to which this research is fully applicable across cultural (and, as we shall see, temporal) contexts.

This, then, is a profile of educationally ambitious Chicanas from one generation, the first wave of the "baby-boomers." But what of the women finishing their educations today? Do low-income Chicanas from a more recent generational cohort respond in the same way to social forces, and have those forces changed appreciably for the women of the 1990s?

WOMEN OF THE SECOND GENERATION

The changing social landscape of the United States over the last decade and a half, including a period of political conservatism with respect to educational and social equity goals, and the increasing visibility of women in a wider range of roles, beckoned the question: How might a more recent cohort of educationally ambitious Chicanas differ from the study's sample of women? To answer this question, a new sample of women was drawn who had completed their graduate educations within the last seven years, that is, between the late 1980s and the present. This new sample of women, which might be called the second generation of educationally ambitious Chicanas, was selected in the same way as the first sample, by contacting key individuals in institutions across the country who were likely to know of recent Chicana graduates, and by asking subjects to nominate other subjects. Just as with the first sample, it was difficult to find women who met the socioeconomic criteria of the study. Now, as then, it is especially difficult for women to make the enormous leap from low-income homes with limited formal education to completing graduate educations in this country. The search lasted several months. Table 7.1 shows the geographic origins, degrees, and the graduate institutions of the new sample compared to the original sample. Table 7.2 shows the demographic profiles of the two samples.

The two samples of women are separated by seventeen years in age; however, with respect to other characteristics they are remarkably similar. Although there are more immigrants in the first sample (meaning these women came here as young children but completed most or all of their elementary and secondary educations in the United States), the combined totals of immigrants and children of immigrants (first generation) is very similar across the two samples. Likewise, while the distribution of fathers who are unskilled and semiskilled (e.g., farm laborers versus truck drivers) differs across the two samples, when these first two categories are combined and contrasted to the skilled laborers (e.g., mechanic, ironworker), whose jobs generally offer greater security and income, the two samples again look very similar. The newer sample also comes from slightly smaller families (fewer siblings) and have parents with marginally more education, both characteristics which could be attributed to the slightly lower percentage of immigrants among the parents and the general increase in education and decrease

TABLE 7.1. *Women's Educational and Occupational Descriptors for Samples I and II*

Subject's Home State	Degree	Graduate Institution	Occupation
SAMPLE I			
California	Ph.D. Social Welfare	Brandeis	Professor
Texas	Ph.D. Linguistics	U of Texas, Austin	Professor
Texas	Ph.D. Spanish	UCLA	Professor
California	Ph.D. Economics	Stanford/UCLA	Researcher
Texas	Ph.D. Counsel Psychology	U of Oregon	Therapist
California	Ph.D. Education	Claremont	Professor
California	Ph.D. Literature	UC San Diego	Professor
California	Ph.D. Anthropology	Stanford	Professor
Texas	Ph.D. Biology	Rutgers	Professor
California	Ph.D. Political Science	UC Riverside	Professor
Texas	J.D.	Georgetown U	Public Interest Lawyer
California	J.D.	UCLA	Public Interest Lawyer
Texas	J.D.	American U	Government Lawyer
Arizona	J.D.	U of Arizona	Public Interest Lawyer
California	J.D.	UC Davis	Corporate Lawyer
Texas	M.D.	UCLA	Physician
California	M.D.	UC Davis	Physician
California	M.D.	UC Davis	Physician
California	M.D.	UC Davis	Physician
California	M.D.	UCLA	Physician
SAMPLE II			
California	Ph.D.Education	Stanford	Professor
Arizona	Ph.D. Spanish	Stanford	Professor
Illinois	Ph.D. Romance Languages	Harvard	Professor
California	Ph.D. Sociology	UC Berkeley	Professor
California	Ph.D. Sociology/Education	Stanford	Professor
Texas	Ph.D. Sociology	Stanford	Professor
California	Ph.D. Economics	Geo Mason University	Professor
Arizona	Ph.D. Rhetoric	U of Colorado	Professor
Texas	Ph.D. Literature	U of Texas, Austin	Professor
Texas	Ph.D. Education	UCLA	Professor
California	J.D.	UC Davis	Public Interest Lawyer
Illinois	J.D.	Boalt	Unemployed
California	J.D.	Boalt	Unemployed
California	J.D.	UC Davis	Corporate Lawyer
California	J.D.	McGeorge	State Government
California	M.D.	U of Southern California	Physician
California	M.D.	UC Davis	Physician
California	M.D.	UC Davis	Physician
California	M.D.	U of Wisconsin	Physician
California	M.D.	UC Irvine	Physician

Table 7.2. *Demographic Profiles of Women for Samples I and II*

	N	Generation			Mean Age	Father or Primary Wage Earner's Occupation			Mean Years of Education		Mother Employed?		Number of Siblings
		Immigrant	First generation	Second generation		Unskilled	Semiskilled	Skilled	Father	Mother	Yes	No	Means
SAMPLE I	20	7 (35%)	8 (40%)	5 (25%)	48	15 (75%)	3 (15%)	2 (10%)	5.2	5.6	13 (65%)	7 (35%)	5.5
SAMPLE II	20	3 (15%)	10 (50%)	7 (35%)	31	8 (40%)	9 (45%)	3 (15%)	6.4	6.3	15 (75%)	5 (25%)	4.9

in family size that has characterized the Mexican American population in United States over this period of time (Grebler, Moore, & Guzmán, 1970; McCarthy & Valdez, 1986; Chapa & Valencia, 1993). For both groups, 65 to 75 percent of mothers were wage earners, contributing to the household support.

To answer the question of how the second generation of educationally ambitious Chicanas might differ from the first, questions focused on the areas which were hypothesized to have been most affected by social change over the last decade and a half: precollege schooling experiences, marriage and family responsibilities, the role of mentors and social support systems, and the importance of recruitment and financial aid. Also of interest was whether the factors associated with home that were so important for the earlier generation continued to play a central role in shaping the aspirations of this newer generation of women.

COMPARING THE TWO SAMPLES

The Similarities

With respect to precollege schooling, the two generations of women attended demographically very similar elementary and secondary schools. Seventy percent of the first generation and 65 percent of the second generation attended public schools. The balance of the women attended Catholic schools for at least three years. When they attended these schools for only a single period of time, it was inevitably during the junior high or middle school years, when parents were exceptionally concerned about keeping their girls "on track." As one young sociologist noted, "it was my mother's philosophy that this was a dangerous time [in a young person's life] to be in public schools." While most of the women attended public schools, in both generations, it is nonetheless significant that about a third attended Catholic schools (this was roughly the same percentage as for the males), inasmuch as only about 11 percent of all students attend nonpublic schools (National Center for Education Statistics, 1991).[1] Given that these individuals came from homes with very modest resources, the percentage of women in Catholic schools must be seen as exceptionally high and an additional indicator of the press for achievement that existed within these subjects' families.

Seventy percent of the second generation Chicanas attended highly mixed or mostly white schools, as did 75 percent of the generation of women

---

1. Interestingly, this figure has fluctuated very little over the last couple decades. Moreover, attendance in nonpublic schools is generally lower in the Southwest United States, where the majority of these individuals grew up, than in other parts of the country (NCES, 1991).

Table 7.3. *Women's High School Racial/Ethnic Composition for Sample I and II*

	All/Almost All Mexican American	Mixed Minority	Mostly Mexican American Significant Number of Anglos	Almost All Anglo	Mixed*
SAMPLE I	4 (20%)	1 (5%)	0 (0%)	12 (60%)	3 (15%)
SAMPLE II	2 (10%)	2 (10%)	2 (10%)	9 (45%)	5 (25%)

* At least 50 percent Anglo, or more than half of schooling experience took place in mostly Anglo schools.

before them (see table 7.3). This is particularly salient in light of the fact that data on racial and ethnic segregation of schools in the population centers where most of these women grew up, in California and Texas, show that fewer than 10 percent of Hispanic students attend highly integrated or mostly white schools (Orfield, Montford, & George, 1987).

Also, like the women who preceded them, 70 percent of these women made their school friendships from among Anglo and other non-Latino schoolmates, since contact with Chicano peers at school was so limited. It is evident that the schools these women attended, and the peer relations they experienced there, were unlike the schools and friendship groups that most Chicanas of their generation and socioeconomic status were experiencing. Across both generations the women commented that this exposure to upwardly mobile white students, usually in the college-prep track, was instrumental in helping them to shape their own ambitions and in providing them with access to information that would be critical to their future educations. One woman who had been tracked into a non-college-preparatory course of study was very clear on how this exposure to non-Chicano students had made the difference for her:

> It was in the band. As a result of being with the white students, having to sit next to them, . . . so I learned a lot about the academic situation and how I wasn't reading Steinbeck, how I wasn't reading novels, and how I wasn't taking the same courses that my peers were taking. And consequently that was real instructive to me, figuring out I had to take chemistry, so I did take that on my own. . . . I would say that had the biggest impact, being in the band and seeing what I wasn't getting from school.

Like the previous generation of women, 60 percent of the second generation women had decided prior to high school that they wanted to go to college. This is interesting in light of the younger women's more uneven academic records. However, most of the women who had decided early were also consistently good students, though three of the women who reported knowing they would go to college even before high school also experienced periods of low academic achievement.

Only one-fourth of these women of the second cohort reported having had a mentor who intervened on their behalf to help them get to college. This is very similar to the 30 percent of the first cohort who reported having had a mentor. The remaining 75 percent of the women commonly received diffuse encouragement, with teachers praising them for being bright and capable, but rarely stepping forward to facilitate their entry into college. One young sociologist expressed her frustration with the lack of mentoring and encouragement she had received throughout her South Texas schooling:

> You know, it's like I always wanted to go to college but I always had a fundamental insecurity about that because . . . no one ever sponsored me or took me under their wing and said, "this is what you do to pursue this career." . . . No one ever did that to me, no one ever saw me as college material. . . . But if you look at me, I should've been sponsored. I was ambitious, you know, I had the drive.

One of the women, a young civil rights lawyer who grew up the daughter of farmworkers in the California central valley, did have a mentor, her uncle, only a few years older than her, who was a high school counselor. She described how critical his intervention was:

> Nobody told me what I needed to do to get into college. The counselors wanted me to go to junior college even though I graduated at the top of my class. But there was no expectation for Chicanas to be going to school. My uncle said, "You have to apply to the state and UC colleges" . . . [he] gave me an idea about what I needed to do, and I filled out the applications. . . . I think because no other Chicanos had gone on to college, they really didn't know what to do with us.

Mentoring and recruitment for graduate level programs did, however, play a significant role for many of the women in choosing to continue their educations beyond the baccalaureate. Most women mentioned someone outside their families who had been instrumental at this point. This person was most often a minority faculty member or program director. For the sociology professor who had never been viewed as "college material," a Chicano professor at the University of Texas was pivotal:

> You know [it was] just the way he dealt with me. He just assumed that I would go on for my doctorate. I kind of looked at him the way he talked to me and I said, "So you think I can, you think that I should?" And he said, "Yeah, I just assumed that you would be going for your doctorate." . . . He had a lot of power because he saw in me what I didn't see in myself. So he ended up being very, very pivotal in terms of pursuing a doctorate.

Almost all of the women also participated in student groups that were geared toward supporting Chicano undergraduate and graduate students, and most commented that these groups had been helpful in keeping them on track and focused academically as well as in providing emotional support. Typical of the comments offered by these women were those of one Ph.D.:

> The Chicana graduate students . . . organization . . . was especially important in graduate school, more than at any other time, because it was so hard. I found comfort and solace around people who were experiencing many of the same things that I was experiencing. Yeah. I couldn't have survived without my network of friends.

Women from the earlier cohort commented as well on the importance of peer support during their graduate educations, and some were very heavily involved in campus politics and ethnic organizations, like the woman who credited this involvement with getting her into graduate school:

> I got involved with a group called La Raza and we started the group in [that city] and we got involved in confrontations with schools of social work in trying to get more Chicanos involved. During one of the meetings that we had with the administration, they said, "We will accept Chicanos, except they have to be qualified," and they went on to explain what they wanted, and we said, "If we find that person would you hire them right now?" and they said, "Yes." Then, my friends said, "You have that person right here," and they hired me on the spot. That is how I got my Master's. . . . and my Ph.D.

Nonetheless, the first cohort, as a whole, was not as involved in such organizations as the second generation. Perhaps this was because Mexican American student organizations were new to many campuses outside of the Southwest during the tenure of the first generation Chicanas, or perhaps it was because these women had been so singlemindedly driven to what was, at that time, an almost impossible goal. Whatever the reason, the second generation Chicanas, as a group, felt their college lives much more intertwined with the Chicano movement than did the first generation. This fact no doubt served them well in maintaining their educational goals intact as they faced many more competing forces than the women who had preceded them. Periods of uneven educational performance, troubled marriages, and young children required that the women seek support for their goals wherever they could find it.

One woman used the experience with a Chicano Rights organization, to which her mentor, a junior-college professor, had introduced her, to build her self-confidence as a woman dealing with "men's issues":

> I joined a group, Community for Chicano Rights, my teacher was a member. They were mostly older men, *muy machistas*, but they

were into struggling to make things better. They took my opinions
seriously, they liked me. All through college I stuck with this group.
It was really good for my self-concept.

Also like the women in the generation before them, the women of the
second sample were most influenced in their educational plans by their
mothers. Eighty percent (16) of these women, exactly the same percentage as
for the first generation, cited their mothers alone or their mother and father
together as the parent with the greatest influence on their educational aspirations. Only three women (15 percent) cited their father as the major influence.
Likewise, most of the mothers of these subjects, like the mothers of the
previous generation, were income-earners and were seen by their daughters
as having powerful roles within the family. Again, like the women before
them, these women report little difference in the degree to which parents
encouraged their sons and their daughters to achieve. Underscoring this is the
fact that no gender pattern is discernible in the college-going behavior of the
siblings in either of the two samples; in some cases only the women in the
family attended and completed college, in other cases all siblings or a mixture
of both brothers and sisters were college-goers.

The Differences

In a major departure from the first generation Chicanas, 40 percent of the
second generation women admitted to having done poorly at school some
time in their precollege careers, receiving low grades (Cs and below) and/or
exhibiting behavioral problems. Interestingly, however, in spite of having a
less illustrious academic record, the same percentage of these women (20
percent) were placed into the lower academic track at some time during high
school as in the first generation sample, suggesting that, for the earlier generation, something may have been operating in these decisions besides the
women's own records or abilities. For the second generation women, those
who had done poorly at one time were, indeed, the ones who were tracked
into the non-college prep track, but not all of the one-time low performers met
that fate. Some were able to talk their way into the college-prep track before
they were assigned to the lower track for which they had been slated. A recent
law school graduate from the second cohort explained how she had coun-
tered the opposition to placing her in college prep courses when she changed
from an all-Chicano to a mostly white high school:

My counselor, when I first signed up for high school there, she
automatically assumed that I was taking Home Ec, that I was going to
be taking all of these . . . needle-type classes, even though I came
from . . . the highest classes. She was like, "Oh, no. You can't

compete with our students." . . . You know, I didn't take Home Ec,
but I had to basically go to a remedial math class before I could go to
algebra when I was already taking algebra! . . . then basically I got
the grades . . . and was put into appropriate classes. You know, I
signed myself up for biology and all that stuff . . . . I had to almost
argue with my counselor to put me in classes.

It is notable that despite a decade and a half of progress on other fronts,
and an increasing awareness of the needs and limitations of low-income and
minority women, so much academic potential was unchanneled by schools
and communities. Moreover, only 35 percent of the women in this sample,
down from 50 percent of the previous cohort, stated that they had had any
contact with college recruitment efforts. The majority had never met a college
recruiter. They did, however, give considerable credit to financial aid programs
for making their educations possible. Only two of the women in this sample
expressed the optimistic view that they would have been able to complete
their undergraduate educations without the loans, grants, and work-study they
received, by scaling back to lower cost institutions and working longer hours.
None of the women believed that graduate education would have been
possible without financial aid.

The second generation of educationally ambitious Chicanas also differed
from the older cohort, as well as non-Hispanic women of their own generation,
in areas of marriage and childbearing. Data for the year 1988 at the University
of California show that 53 percent of women were married at the time they
completed their doctoral educations (California Postsecondary Education
Commission, 1990). This compares to only 15 percent of this sample who were
married. Five additional women, all Ph.D's, had been married during their
undergraduate educations and into their graduate schooling, but all of these
women had divorced prior to completing their degrees. Four of the women
had had children during their college years. This represents a substantial
departure from the pattern of the first generation women, all of whom waited
until late in their educations to marry, if at all, none of whom had divorced at
the same point in their careers, and none of whom had children until they were
nearing completion of their graduate degrees.

Another difference between the two groups was found in the way they
accounted for their academic accomplishments. Whereas the earlier sample
tended to attribute their achievements to the help and support of others, more
than half of this sample of women found the source of their accomplishments
within themselves or considered them a manifestation of their desires to "set
an example" or be "socially responsible." Again, the women of this second
cohort appear to be moving closer to the norm for all academically ambitious
women and men, even in their self-evaluations.

Finally, the new sample of women was asked to reflect on the difference it might have made had they not been women. Four of the women, or 20 percent, either felt that it would not have made any difference or could not envision how things would have been different. The majority of the women, however, felt that their career paths might have taken quite different turns; they would have felt less discrimination in their fields and several felt they might have gone into a different field altogether—one they believed had been foreclosed to them by their gender.

SUMMARY

What, then, are the enduring characteristics of these educationally ambitious Mexican American women across two generations? For the most part they came from families that were exceptionally supportive of their educational goals, given the parents' limited resources and lack of experience with education. Even in the poorest families there were almost invariably dictionaries and encyclopedias, and most had a daily newspaper. Moreover, most parents tended to encourage their sons and daughters equally, although there is some evidence that they were more specific with, and offered more alternatives to, their sons. Mothers within these families were strong figures who typically contributed to the household support with their own earnings.

Across both generations, the women disproportionately attended highly mixed or mostly white schools and had extensive contact with nonminority peers. These peer contacts helped, in part, to compensate for the lack of early mentoring that these women experienced. Furthermore, 20 percent of the women in both groups were placed in non-college-preparatory tracks and had to argue their way into the college-prep track in high school.

In what ways do the two generations differ? Perhaps happily, the second generation of women does not appear to exhibit quite the same "Superwoman" syndrome of the previous generation. There was a little more margin for error in their lives. Several of these women had gotten "off track" for a period of time and were able to recover without seriously jeopardizing their educational futures. The fact that more of the second generation women had also married and had children prior to completing their studies suggests that, as a group, these Chicanas may be approaching a more typical female life pattern. The fact that half of the new sample of Ph.D.'s had married and divorced prior to the completion of their degrees also suggests that role redefinitions, and the stresses on these women, may have been great.

How these women were able to resist the culture of romance and maintain their educational ambitions is, however, less than clear. Involvement in ethnic and academic organizations that transmitted a message of doing well in order to benefit one's community was certainly important, but it could not fully explain these women's successful resistance. Perhaps American society is changing rapidly enough that women of all backgrounds are coming to see their options as less a function of their gender than of their own yearnings. Surely, though, the example of strong mothers who admonished them not to depend on a man to make their way in the world, and who "wanted it all" for their daughters, was a powerful weapon against patriarchal hegemony in this generation as well as in the last.

Unhappily, the second generation women had benefitted less from college recruitment activities and had to rely more on their own resources to find their way onto a university campus. Financial aid was noted as having been even more critical to these women than to the earlier generation; the rising cost of education was frequently cited as the reason for this enhanced significance. It is entirely possible that the earlier generation of women was less concerned about costs, however, because they received more support in scholarships and grants associated with the active recruitment from which they had benefited.

CONCLUSIONS

The portrait of the kinds of families and schools that are producing educationally ambitious Chicanas from the lower and working classes is relatively stable over time. In spite of their limited resources, these women's family and schooling experiences were much like those reported in the literature for middle class and male achievers, with a couple of important exceptions: tracking and mentoring.

Academic tracking experiences were consistent across the two female cohorts: more than one-fourth were not slated for the college-bound track in their high schools. This was in spite of the fact that all of the women were good students and most had demonstrated outstanding academic performance in the classroom. Moreover, they were much better students than the men who had been tracked into non-college-prep courses in only marginally higher proportions (37 percent). In the schools where there was a college-bound track, all of the women eventually made it in, and this became a critical element in their future academic endeavors.

Women also differed from men in the extent to which they were mentored during their precollege years. Approximately two-thirds of the women reported having had no mentors in spite of the fact that they represented such extraordinary potential. This is in contrast to the earlier sample of males, two-thirds of whom reported being the recipients of mentoring experiences.

Differences do appear between the two female cohorts in their contact with college recruitment efforts. In contrast to the earlier group of women, half of whom attributed their college attendance to some aspect of recruiting, only one-third of the second generation women had had such an experience. This fact is telling when considering that they should have represented precisely the ideal target for any recruitment effort: Mexican American women from low income backgrounds with good academic records.

Finally, it is notable that among the forty women for whom the country was scoured, there is not one Ph.D. in engineering, physical science, or mathematics, nor among the physicians is there a surgeon. These women were largely attracted to the same fields to which women in general have traditionally gravitated. A number of women, when asked whether their educational careers would have been any different if they hadn't been women, suggested that perhaps they would have pursued a more "technical" field or perhaps their parents would have encouraged them into something more "nontraditional." One woman gave a particularly insightful response:

> If I had been born male I probably would not have done as well because I would have resisted. I was able to put up with more; as a female, I accepted humiliation more.

Several of the women simply could not answer this question. This fact, alone, is testimony to the impact of the women's movement on these women's lives. But the miniscule numbers of Chicanas from the lower and working classes who manage to complete doctoral work, and their ghettoization into more traditional "women's fields," suggests that the road to equality of educational opportunity is still a long one.

EIGHT

Summary and Conclusions

In spite of serious economic disadvantage, most of these subjects' parents were doing precisely the kinds of things that the literature reports are important for instilling achievement motivation in children, but which are generally believed to be restricted to the middle class. For the most part, they (especially the mothers) were very supportive of their children's educational goals, set high performance standards, modeled and encouraged literacy, and helped with schoolwork in any way they could. Many of the parents also facilitated their children's attendance in schools outside their neighborhoods that were perceived to be better than the schools to which their children had been assigned.

One difference between these parents and the parents of middle-class achievers, however, was in their parenting styles. Relatively few of these parents were characterized as being "authoritative," the warm and democratic approach demonstrated in the literature to encourage both independence and high aspirations. These parents were more commonly authoritarian, laying down rigid rules with little discussion, a style that is believed to undermine a sense of independence and self-efficacy in children. Why, then, did this style of parenting not have the predicted effect on these subjects? Perhaps because independence was already being reinforced in more tangible ways through an expectation, as one subject put it, that "everyone carries his own load." Or it may be that authoritative parenting requires not only a more enlightened parent but also a more hospitable environment. The rules these parents set were often used to counteract the potentially negative effects of the neighborhoods in which they lived. Subjects were expected to be engaged in productive work and were seldom allowed to just "hang out" with friends in the neighborhood.

Another important difference between these parents and middle-class parents may have been in the way they modeled a hard work ethic. Because of the nature of their work, subjects were very aware of the kind of work their parents did (many of the subjects worked alongside their parents) and the near legendary way in which they performed this work. Subjects were clear and consistent in believing that hard work was highly valued within their homes. Although almost one-third of the sample had lived in the United States for two generations or more, these families behaved very much like recent immigrants in their transmission of a hard work/education-as-a-mobility-strategy ethic (Duran & Weffer, 1992; Portes & Rumbaut, 1994).

How does one account for the tremendous press for achievement that existed in most of these homes? I believe the answer lies, in part, in the family stories. Parents told stories of wealth, prestige, and position to their children to keep alive their hopes for a better future. If one has always been poor and one sees nothing but poverty in one's environs, it is probably quite easy to conclude that this is one's destiny. However, if one lives with stories about former exploits, about ancestors who owned their own lands and controlled their own lives, it is probably much easier to imagine that this is one's destiny. At the very least, the evidence exists that, by virtue of family history, one is capable of a better life. Some psychologists have suggested that cultural myths and fairy tales can affect the achievement orientations of an entire populace (see Simonton, 1987), and others (Coles, 1989) have proposed that stories and myths may help weave the moral fabric of a nation's youth; therefore, it would seem a small step to hypothesize that family stories and legends might have had an equally powerful effect on the achievement motivation of these individuals.

In sum, the parents of these subjects created, through the stories and through their own faith in the future exemplified by their own strivings, a *culture of possibility*. And, in so doing, they reinforced in their children a self-belief of efficacy which resulted in intense achievement motivation. In spite of daily evidence to the contrary, these individuals grew up believing they did not have to lead the lives of their parents and others they saw around them. For them, anything was possible, and perhaps even *destined*, as Adrián, the corporate lawyer had indicated when he said he "knew he was destined for something extraordinary."

Beyond the effects of parental press for achievement, or perhaps because of it, subjects expressed intense personal drives for achievement, oftentimes manifested in comments to the effect that they had vowed they would not live in the kind of poverty into which they had been born. Other studies of exceptionally successful or eminent individuals have concluded that some portion of the variance in achievement behavior is probably attributable to genetic inheritance, inborn drives, or inherent personality characteristics (Goertzel, Goertzel, & Goertzel, 1978; Simonton, 1987). These subjects, too, often comment on this inner drive. Typical of the responses to the question "Why were you so educationally successful when other Chicanos in your situation are not?" were such things as "Motivation. I wanted it badly. The need creates a will." Or "Why me? I think because I wanted it more than anybody else." It is difficult to separate the concept of an "inner drive" from the socialization these individuals received at the hands of parents who were so engaged in helping their children to envision a different kind of life than their own. Yet, one suspects that even the "inner drives" were shaped and nurtured in these aspirationally rich home environments.

When asked what personal characteristic made it possible for them to realize their high aspirations, more than two-thirds of the sample cited the most important characteristic as being persistence, not innate ability. In fact, ability was ranked third behind persistence and hard work[1] as a factor in their achievement. Most people saw themselves, like their parents, as extremely hard workers who believed in the promise that anything was possible with enough hard work. Hence, the characteristics of "inner drive" and "persistence," which some researchers have interpreted as "innate," were inextricably bound up in the models set by the parents and the messages they conveyed to their children, both directly and through the family stories.

Parental support, persistence, and some adequate level of ability still would not have been sufficient if these subjects had not also met with opportunity. And it is this area that no doubt holds the greatest promise for educational policy initiatives. Two kinds of opportunity were key: (1) the opportunity to prepare themselves for college by participating in a college-preparatory curriculum, and (2) the information and resources that would make a college education a realizable goal.

Getting tracked into the college-preparatory curriculum did not come easily for many of these subjects. In spite of their enormous potential, almost one-third of the subjects were initially destined for vocational or general education courses which could have effectively foreclosed the opportunity to go to college. One subject, a university professor, recounted poignantly how close she came to missing this critical opportunity and how an accident of course scheduling was instrumental in shaping her aspirations:

> One teacher had an amazing impact on me. . . . She had always taught honors, and she ended up with us, and this class was a mistake. We got assigned to her and we weren't honors students, and she was mad. She let us know the first day of class that there was a mistake and she was going to do everything in her power to change it. So she hoped that within two or three weeks we would have a different teacher. We were all scared. It was hard. Quiet. Silent.

---

1. The personal characteristics reported most often by subjects as being critical to their educational successes, in rank order were: persistence, hard work, ability, clear goals ("knew what I wanted") and interpersonal skills. Each was mentioned by at least 10 percent of the sample.

> She couldn't get her schedule fixed . . . and so she came in and
> said, "Well I'm not going to teach this class any different than I would
> an honors class." And so we were all on our best behavior, it was just
> kind of set up that we had to prove ourselves. It was a literature
> course, that led to my interest in English. We read Wordsworth,
> Thoreau, and Emerson, and . . . I made As in that course and she
> liked me a lot. And she encouraged me. She didn't tell me to go to
> college, she just said, "You're diligent."

> I don't know if she would remember . . . the psychological
> damage, but it all worked out anyway for all of us. We were all great
> students . . . [it] just had that effect, that she didn't alter the course for
> us. We had to recite poetry and we had to learn MacBeth, Hamlet . . .
> and that's what they had to do in honors class.

Once subjects were tracked into the college-prep curriculum, they were invariably exposed to a high-achieving peer group against whom they could test their skills and feel validated by their own performance. These high-achieving peers also helped to keep them "on track" academically, even in the face of other competing peer values. The fact that almost all of these subjects had extensive exposure to middle class and white students also provided the opportunity to learn to move easily between different cultures and to adapt to widely differing situations.

All of these subjects came from low-income backgrounds—this was one of the criteria for inclusion in the study. As such, all had a need for financial support in order to attend college. They also came from homes in which parents had low levels of education; the mean number of years of education completed by mothers and fathers was between four and five. Parents were not in a position to inform their children about college options and opportunities; this information came to them through older siblings who had already been to college, through peers, and through the schools. Over half of the subjects (52 percent) attributed their college and/or graduate school attendance, at least in part, to recruitment programs for Chicanos; programs that brought both information and financial aid. One-third of the subjects used the junior colleges as their entry point into higher education (the percentage was virtually identical for males and females), lacking adequate financial support to go directly to the university.

These subjects attended college during a period when opportunities were opening up for minorities. Major civil rights legislation had recently passed and colleges and universities were recruiting minority applicants and, in many cases, funding their educations. And, after 1965, the federal government began to commit large amounts of aid directly to students in an effort to stimulate an increase in higher-education participation among lower income students

(Astin, 1982). The importance of the time cannot be overstated. Only once before in the history of the United States had such extraordinary opportunities opened up for a single category of citizens, and that was the result of the post–World War II GI Bill which brought unprecedented numbers of first-time students into higher education (Olson, 1974).

One subject commented on the difference the availability of financial aid had made for him, as opposed to his older brother:

> It was 1968, the first or second year that financial assistance was available. Had that not presented itself, I probably would have gone to city college. That's what my brother did; it took him eight years to get a B.A. from the state university. Availability of financial aid was really, really important. What I got from Harvard was more than my dad earned all year.

This subject ended up getting a B.A. and a law degree from Harvard in less time than it took his brother to complete his undergraduate education at the state university while working at the same time. The brother did not pursue any further postsecondary education.

Of course, for all of these subjects, finding a means for financing their educations was extremely important—their families were rarely able to provide financial support. But the social climate that supported programs that reached out to students was also an important factor in their continued education. Many subjects commented that college and university recruiters made the difference between possibility and reality in their college aspirations:

> At that time the Educational Opportunities Program was just being developed. It was the first year that the program was going to go fully into effect. . . . [The recruiter's] first question was, "Do you want to come to UCLA?" And I had never been asked that before. It was more like, "Why should we admit you?" . . . I spent four hours talking to this guy. It was a very different approach and I got so enthusiastic about it, I immediately went home and . . . I decided to go to UCLA.

In spite of the fact that the great majority of these subjects were outstanding students and would have been competitive for admission to the universities they attended under any circumstances, many saw the special minority recruitment programs that opened up for them as key to their higher education. The daughter of cannery workers who had always excelled in school mused:

> It was a good time to come along in the educational system . . . there were opportunities and I either reached for them or stumbled on them. . . . I don't know, I was lucky. If there weren't the opportunities I don't know if I'd be a doctor.

Another subject, who eventually completed medical school, talked about his decision to go to college:

> I went through high school and never really thought of going to college. . . . I thought I was going to be working with the trucks, with my dad. . . . But I got a scholarship . . . and my dad said, "I'm relieving you of all responsibilities for helping support the family." He said, "Go to college, but you're going to have to do it on your own." So I did. I had three jobs.

The role of structured opportunity, whether it was financial aid which became available in large quantity through the federal government, or special recruitment programs, was critical to these subjects. Clearly, they were ambitious, hardworking, even driven to succeed, and most had outstanding academic records—valedictorians, top 10 percent of their classes—but, without someone interceding at the right moment, by their own admission, many probably would not have followed the educational paths they did. One can speculate that because of their ambition and acculturation to hard work, they might well have been even more "successful" in other endeavors, but the question remains open whether they would have been able to find the way to make education their vehicle of mobility. Given the declining percentages of Chicano students going on to college as financial aid has become less available and recruitment efforts have slowed down (Orfield, 1990; Orfield & Paul, 1988), there is some evidence that they would not. Moreover, Post (1990) has demonstrated, with a more recent sample of Chicano high school seniors, that lack of accurate information about college costs and payment options works as a substantial deterrent to college enrollment for Mexican American students. Without renewed intervention, similar to that which provided the stepladder boosting these fifty individuals over the ivy walls, there is every reason to believe that the next generation of Chicanos will find the barriers to elite educations even higher.

NINE

Lessons for School Reform

The group of subjects for this study represents a cohort of individuals who went through college and graduate education during the period of highest participation of minority students on record. It is not the most recent group of graduates. Hence, this group may differ in some ways from those students who are currently on course for graduate study or who have recently completed their graduate educations. We have tested this possibility with a second female sample in chapter 7. However, the research literature up to the present (and including this study) continues to identify the same kinds of factors in high academic achievement that it has for the past several decades. It appears that some things do not change. What does change, however, is the social climate in which aspirations are nurtured or dampened. And because social climate is a human construction, those factors which yield particular social benefit are within our ability, as a society, to modify or create.

Historically, the high academic achievement of people from poverty backgrounds is a relatively new phenomenon, and one that is very much rooted in the American experience. State colleges and universities, as well as a number of very prestigious private institutions, figured heavily into the opportunities provided to these subjects. In fact, when asked to what she attributed her extraordinary accomplishments, one subject replied, "Luck and Princeton!" However, the groundwork for the realization of all of this potential was laid in the mostly public elementary and secondary schools which these subjects attended. What lessons can be learned from these individuals that might be applied to another generation caught in a period of national introspection and education reform? I think there are many.

NURTURING LITERACY

Instructional policy for language-minority students in this country, and in the individual states, has varied according to the ebb and flow of public attitudes toward immigration over the last century. Programs which encouraged the development of children's native languages have flourished in times and places when these immigrants and their languages were perceived as holding little threat to the general welfare (Schlossman, 1983). At other times, and in different places, where language-minority groups have been perceived as too numerous and not rapid enough in assimilating into the American mainstream, strict prohibitions against the instruction and use of a language other than English have been instituted in the public schools, to the extent that parents have been admonished against using their primary language in the home (Carter, 1970; Cummins, 1981).

We now know that literacy, broadly defined as exposure not only to the printed word but to the value of words, discussion, verbal exchange and information, is the key to academic engagement, in whatever language. And families can best nurture literacy in the language in which they are most comfortable and proficient. In fact, it is difficult to imagine nurturing a love of language and the printed word in an idiom one only partially comprehends, or in which one has never read. Yet language policy in the schools has demanded exactly this of many Mexican and Chicano parents.

Most of the subjects of this study spoke Spanish in their homes, most of their parents read in Spanish, and most of the parents, and often older siblings, modeled a love of the written word and an appreciation for the power of knowledge. In most of these homes, in which the next meal was not always a certainty, there was an encyclopedia. For the lawyers and the academics, and especially the women, literacy was a powerful force in their upbringing. What if their parents had heeded the advice of many school personnel and not had the discussions about politics and history in Spanish, not read the Bible in Spanish, not talked about books and operas in Spanish?

Education reform must include in its agenda a policy of bolstering literacy in the homes of Chicano children in the language in which these families are most proficient, knowing that literacy in any language will translate into achievement in English.

DESEGREGATION POLICY

As urban areas around the country have been abandoned by the middle-class and white residents who formerly inhabited them, efforts to desegregate many school districts have been stymied. Recent court decisions as well as public discussion have turned to the idea of strengthening racially segregated schools rather than dwelling on the difficult task of desegregating them. And, many responsible educators have advocated putting resources that might otherwise be devoted to desegregation efforts into building high-quality, all-minority schools, arguing that the critical variable is school excellence, not the students' racial or ethnic mix. Bilingual educators have also worried over the need to maintain a critical mass of limited-English-proficient students in a single language at the same school site in order to provide adequate primary-language instruction. These are both important goals, but the data from this study point to exercising great caution in creating or maintaining all-minority environments, at least for Chicano students.

Excellent minority schools may equip students with the skills they need to continue their educations beyond high school, but they will not provide the validation that comes with competing in an arena that mirrors the society into which they will be thrust. Neither do such homogeneous settings prepare students to move gracefully between one social context and another, as any successful inhabitant of twenty-first-century North America will need to do. These subjects commented repeatedly on how their self-concept was enhanced by knowing they could compete successfully against students whom they had viewed as being models of achievement. It was this knowledge and confidence that made it possible for them to imagine themselves in a world-class university. Moreover, there is considerable evidence that moving back and forth between the two cultures of home peer-groups and school peer-groups provided important adaptive skills that increased their chances of persisting in school.

Although to a large degree decisions about school desegregation have been the purview of the federal courts, education reformers must not remain silent on this issue. Local and state education policies can, and some would argue should, address the need and the wisdom of providing racially and ethnically integrating experiences as part of the school curriculum. Not that this has ever been easy, or that our best efforts have been rewarded with great success. Recent accounts of "resegregation" within ostensibly desegregated schools continue to challenge our concepts of integrated education, as exemplified in a recent ethnographic study of an urban Northern California junior high school:

> "Coolidge" Middle School is located in a middle-class Asian and European American neighborhood. Due to a court order to desegregate in 1983, Coolidge receives about 300 [of its 1400] students who are bussed in from both the Latino district and one of [the district's] African American neighborhoods. . . . The Gifted and Talented program was predominantly Asian and European American; the Special Education program was disproportionately African American. Over one-third of the Latino students at Coolidge were enrolled in ESL [located in separate bungalows minutes from the campus] or Special Ed. These figures show why Coolidge was characterized by educators as "apartheid." (Weinberg, 1994, pp. 9–10.)

Perhaps the linkages will occur over fiberoptic cables rather than bus routes, but the evidence suggests that minority students, and in this case Chicano students, are advantaged by sitting next to students who consider it their birthright to go on to college.

EARLY IDENTIFICATION OF "GIFTED" STUDENTS

There is currently a great emphasis on early intervention with youth "at risk." Such early intervention strategies often include the identification of high-potential students early in their school years in order to provide them with special support to ensure their school success. While this is no doubt helpful to those students who are targeted, many of the subjects of this study, who passed the most stringent post hoc criterion for being "high potential," would not have been so identified early in their school careers. Ten percent of these subjects would not have been considered "college material" until their senior year of high school, or later. More than half of the sample reported doing poorly in school at some point—for the women this was early in their schooling and due to language factors. But for the men, many had uneven profiles of achievement, doing well during one time, then poorly during another. Depending on when the identification is done—and there would have been no consistently good time to do it with this sample—up to half of these proven achievers would have been missed in the screening.

For students with stable social and economic backgrounds who are not dealing with issues of development, discrimination, and stereotyping, it may be statistically defensible to attempt to identify high potential early and nurture it. For Chicano students with backgrounds similar to those in this study, it would seem wiser to assume that all have high potential and nurture all equally.

REWARDING EFFORT AND PERSISTENCE

In a related vein, the self-assessment by subjects that persistence and effort were what accounted for their extraordinary academic attainments, not innate ability, sends a powerful message to our schools which often function as little more than a "meritocratic" sorting device. While the American educational system is no doubt the most open in the world with respect to providing access, there is something in the American ethos which precludes higher academic attainment more powerfully than structural barriers. This is the belief, however unspoken, in the salience of ability over effort, which results in our willingness to turn over the futures of our children to the assumed predictive ability of standardized tests.

Twenty percent of the study subjects reported that they had actually been placed in non-college-preparatory tracks at some time during high school, usually on the basis of an ability or aptitude test that they had been given. Another five subjects (10 percent) recounted how they had had to argue on their own behalf to avoid placement in these same lower-track classes to which they were originally scheduled. Even in the face of high academic achievement, counselors continued to place more faith in the test scores than they did in the subjects' performance. These are not isolated cases.

Stevenson and Stigler (1992) report on American, Chinese, and Japanese mothers' perceptions of the reasons for their children's academic performance. By a substantial margin, American mothers tended to attribute their children's school performance to ability rather than effort. In contrast, both the Chinese and Japanese mothers made the reverse attributions. Moreover, American mothers were more satisfied with their children's achievement, at whatever level, than were the Asian mothers, assumedly because they perceived that their children were doing the best they could.

As long as we allow notions of fixed ability to override our emphasis on effort and hard work, on the part of both students and teachers, we are likely to misidentify a substantial portion of our high-potential minority students and miss the opportunity to empower teachers to change children's futures, not just rubberstamp them. As standards are ratcheted upward in the effort to raise the level of achievement for all students, education reformers and teacher educators must find ways to reward students for their efforts. Not in the sense of passing them on because they have tried, even though they have failed the material, but in being willing to hang in there with them while they spend more time on the material that hasn't yet been mastered.

One well-known teacher who has had extraordinary success with Chicano students from low-income backgrounds tells his high school administration, "Don't send me 'gifted' kids, I want kids who want to become gifted. In my class they will become gifted!" Then, he asks the students, "Who wants to study? Who wants to work hard? Who wants a ticket to college?" Into this self-selected group fall many students who other teachers have written off because of low grades or test scores. And, incredibly, they "become gifted," not by fiat but by investing more time and effort in the subject matter than other students.

Assessment will no doubt command a larger and larger role in our education reform efforts; it is important to monitor the progress of our efforts. Nonetheless we must find ways to monitor without pre-sorting. Testing and assessment of *individual* students must be reconceptualized as diagnostic, not predictive, and a student's, and family's, willingness to put forth effort should always be the primary factor in awarding opportunity. This is an important principle for all students, but it becomes especially key for Chicano students who have been tripped up time and again by formal and informal assessments that have plainly underestimated their potential.

REANALYZING AND RETHINKING "TRACKING"

All of these subjects were eventually placed in college-preparatory tracks in high school. For them it worked to their advantage. Had they not been so placed it is virtually certain that they would not have been eligible for the educational opportunities they were to be offered. But, it is also further evidence of the powerful effects of tracking. By being placed in these tracks, students who came from backgrounds which *should have* been predictive of academic failure were able to beat the odds; by being labeled "smart" they came to believe that they were, and by being grouped with other similarly labeled students they were exposed to a curriculum and set of standards that made their college educations possible. Also, by being placed in this track, information and opportunities were made available to them that most Chicano students never knew existed. For the lucky few who make it into the college-bound track, the rewards are considerable, but one has to wonder how many were missed along the way.

There is a hint of the numbers of students who are no doubt lost in the system in some of the stories told by these subjects: the sociologist who "discovered" that a college-bound track existed by sitting next to band members who were reading books she had never heard of; the lawyer who produced evidence that she had been the valedictorian of her eighth-grade class in an initially unsuccessful attempt to be placed into college-prep classes; the science professor who was told by his high school counselor that he shouldn't aspire beyond vocational courses at the local junior college.

The whole issue of academic tracking is more complex than educators have fully acknowledged. Its evils have been painfully documented in ways that have caused many to renounce it as a policy, at the same time that teachers, pointing out their frustration in trying to teach algebra to students who cannot add, have caused these same educators to rethink their renunciations.

Tracking works. It worked for these subjects; it provided the environment, the encouragement, the peer group, the subject-matter knowledge, and the real-world information that was critical in propelling them forward. It also isolated them to some extent from peers who were headed down a different path. Had these subjects been heterogeneously grouped with their neighborhood peers, it is entirely possible that their life and academic choices would have been quite different. Yet, they represent only a tiny percentage of their social and economic peers, and, by their own admissions, they were often not the brightest stars, even in their own local galaxies.

Education reform must grapple with the conundrum of academic tracking and find a way to wrap at-risk students who aspire to a different future in a protective college-bound cocoon, while still providing access to these same opportunities for students who may not yet know they want to, or are capable of, reaching that far.

SCHOOL CHOICE

The issue of school choice has been brought to the educational policy table in recent times by Republican administrations at both the state and federal levels. The failure of the Republicans to capture the 1992 election and the defeat of several key state proposals certainly stalled the momentum of the school-choice movement but no means squelched it. A number of prominent and thoughtful educational researchers and practitioners have called for a non-partisan review of different kinds of choice mechanisms. Given the chronic low level of achievement in many inner-city schools and among many poor and minority children, the issue is not likely to go away. Nor should it. In spite of poverty conditions, one-third of this sample of high achieving Chicanos had been placed in nonpublic schools by parents who were concerned about what their local schools could offer. Others had moved to new neighborhoods or manipulated their attendance at "better" public schools by exercising other options. There is also evidence that many of these subjects had lived in "frontier" or fringe areas of the barrio that had afforded them more and better choices in schooling than were available to most Chicano families.

Although they lived in highly segregated neighborhoods, and most grew up in the Southwest where all-Chicano schools are common, almost two-thirds of these subjects attended mostly white and ethnically mixed schools. Additional data on a group of women who have completed their educations more recently suggests that this factor may have become even more pronounced, in spite of the fact that segregation has increased for Chicanos over the last two decades (Chapa & Valencia, 1993).

Educationally ambitious Chicano families are evidently making their own school choices, even within what must be considered very restricted circumstances. To the extent that public schools serving the nation's barrios do not provide an education equal to that of more middle class neighborhoods, there is every reason to believe that the most ambitious Chicano students, regardless of income, will find alternative schools, further eroding the barrio schools' academic strength.

Education reform efforts must pay attention to the distribution of opportunity among schools in low-income areas if they are to have any holding power with the most educationally ambitious Chicano students and any hope of reaching the less ambitious.

REFOCUSING THE RESEARCH LENS

Much of what we do in the name of education reform is based on social-science research. Many of our own opinions, as well, are shaped by our reading of the research. But, when that research falls short, or is over-generalized, it can lead us to policies and practices that not only fail to help students, but, indeed, harm them. One such example was the research conducted during the the 1940s and 1950s on bilingualism. These studies, by correlating student achievement with a loosely defined trait called bilingualism, and failing to take into account a host of mediating variables, concluded that bilingualism was, in and of itself, responsible for academic retardation in children (Darcy, 1953). As a result, for at least two decades North American teachers routinely admonished parents against raising their children bilingually or using the parents' primary language in the home with the children. We can only now begin to speculate on the enormous damage that this piece of advice has wrought on at least one generation of learners.

Much of the research reviewed for this study has implications for education reform measures. But, most of the conclusions that have been drawn from this research have never considered the implications for children other than those on whom it was conducted: typically white, middle-class students, and often males. Hence, we know that particular parenting styles are correlated with higher academic achievement in children, but we are not sure if this works in the same way for Chicano children. Some evidence in this study suggests that it may not. We know that low-performing peers do have negative effects on students' academic orientations, but it is unclear if this operates in the same way for Chicano students. This study suggests that even low-performing Chicano peers may play a role in supporting high academic achievement, under certain conditions. We know that, statistically, the particular school a student attends contributes only slightly to explaining the variance in student achievement, but this study suggests that for some Chicano students, the schools they attend may be critical in helping to shape their aspirations.

This same kind of social-science knowledge affects the way we see the potential of students. We *know* that parents who are involved in their children's schools and who attend school events and teacher conferences are more likely to have children who do well. Many of the parents of the high-achieving Chicanos of this sample, however, never visited their children's schools, some never even showed up for parent conferences. We have also come to believe, through the social-science literature, that in Mexican and Chicano families women play a subservient role to men and that most decision-making falls within the males' domain. These subjects overwhelmingly had powerful mothers who were income-earners and decision-makers in their own homes. They were also, most often, the impetus behind their children's strivings.

These are all examples of research-based knowledge that could lead us to formal educational policies and informal educational decisions that might be as disastrous as the belief that bilingualism is an educational handicap. As the school-reform agenda continues to unfold across the nation, it behooves us all to remind ourselves that policies for the future should not be based on what we "know" from research done with subjects and under conditions that may bear little resemblance to a rapidly changing present.

Appendix

The following represent the question areas posed to the subjects. Where greater precision was required in order to make comparisons between subjects and others to whom they were comparing themselves, respondents were requested to quantify their answers on a scale, usually from one to five, which was anchored with a descriptor at each point. However, the interviews were conversational in nature and respondents were allowed to digress and expand upon areas that are not directly touched by the questions. Hence, information about respondents' experiences exceeds the specific questions that are posed here as stimulus prompts. The following questions represent the framework for the interview and indicate a minimum level of data collected.

Items marked with an asterisk were included in the data collection instrument for the sample II women reported on in Chapter 7, in addition to the six new questions listed on page 133 of the Appendix.

Demographic/background information

* *1. Birthdate
* 2. Gender
* *3. Place of birth
* *4. Did subject attend preschool/kindergarten?
* *5. Names and locations of all elementary, junior high/middle and high schools and whether they were public, private, or parochial.
* *6. College(s) and graduate school(s) attended, years attended, locations, and degrees awarded, financial considerations.
* *7. How did respondents find out about colleges.
* *8. Current occupation and marital status.

127

9. Where parents were born.

10. Where grandparents were born (both grandparents on both sides of the family).

*11. Reasons all family members gave for immigrating to the United States.

*12. Generation of the respondent.

13. Amount of contact/travel to Mexico.

*14. Father's occupation while respondent was growing up (until respondent finished high school).

*15. Highest grade in school completed by father.

*16. Mother's occupation while respondent was growing up (until respondent finished high school).

*17. Highest grade completed by mother.

18. Age of both parents at birth of respondent.

19. Composition of family at the time respondent finished high school (was original family intact—if not, at what point did change occur?)

*20. List of all siblings, ages, gender, current occupation and schooling.

*21. Number of sibs with B.A. or above.

*22. Birth order of the respondent.

*23. Language(s) spoken in the home with (a) mother (b) father (c) sibs (d) others.

*24. Which language respondent spoke primarily when beginning school.

*25. How language use changed over time.

Religion

1. Religion practiced during formative years.
2. Level of religiousness of family (scale of 1 to 5).
3. Kinds of church activities in which respondent participated.
4. Regularity of attendance at church services.
5. The role that religion played in the family.
6. The role that religion has played in the life of the respondent and the role it may have played in the formation of career/educational goals.

Mentors

*1. Person(s) who influenced the respondent most in setting educational goals.

Childrearing practices and parental characteristics

*1. Which parent had greatest influence on the development of educational goals.

*2. Mother's attitudes toward the value of education (scale of 1 to 5).

*3. Father's attitudes toward the value of education (scale of 1 to 5).

*4. Other influential person's (name) attitudes toward the value of education (scale of 1 to 5).

*5. In what specific ways did parents assist in early schooling (preparing the respondent for schooling).

*6. Were financial sacrifices ever made to assist in schooling.

7. Style of discipline exercised by father (authoritative, authoritarian, or permissive—each explained).

8. Style of discipline exercised by mother (authoritative, authoritarian, or permissive—each explained).

9. Characteristics mother valued most in her children.

*10. How much education mother *hoped* respondent would complete.

*11. How much education mother *expected* respondent would complete.

12. Characteristics father valued most in his children.

*13. How much education father *hoped* respondent would complete.

*14. How much education father *expected* respondent would complete.

15. What "getting ahead" or "being successful" meant to mother.

16. What "getting ahead' or "being successful" meant to father.

*17. Occupations suggested by mother.

*18. Occupations suggested by father.

19. Discussion of current events, news, community issues and politics in the family: How often. Who initiated the conversations.

20. How highly valued was individual independence or self-reliance in the family (scale of 1 to 5).

21. Importance of familial independence of others (scale of 1 to 5).

22. In what ways did parents encourage independence.

23. In comparison to other children in the neighborhood, did respondent have more or less freedom to go places and decide own activities (scale of 1 to 5).

*24. Importance of work responsibilities in elementary school.

*25. Importance of work responsibilities in high school.

26. Specific responsibilities (outside of school) required of the respondent at age 12.

27. Compared to other children respondent knew, were these responsibilities greater or less in elementary school (scale of 1 to 5).

28. Compared to other children respondent knew, were these responsibilities greater or less in high school (scale of 1 to 5).

29. Special hobbies that either parent pursued.

30. Cultural activities that either parent engaged in (music, dance, art, literature, etc.)
*31. Did either parent read a great deal. What did they read.
32. Mother's involvement in activities outside the home (including church, clubs, civic, trade unions, etc.)
33. Father's involvement in activities outside the home (including church, clubs, civic, trade unions, etc.)
34. Parent with greatest influence on family decisions/Parent with the dominant personality.
35. Was home harmonious.
36. Was idea of "standing up for your rights" a particular characteristic of either parent.
37. Compared to the respondent's peers, were standards parents set for behavior and school performance higher or lower than those set by peers' parents (scale of 1 to 5).
38. Did parents ever discourage playing/spending time with other children in the neighborhood.
39. Did parents view selves as different from other families in the neighborhood. In what ways.
40. Did parents ever indicate that respondent was "different" from peers or sibs in regard to ability or potential?
41. Family cohesiveness. Frequency with which family did things together (scale of 1 to 5).
42. Types of activities that family engaged in together.
43. Who signed respondent's report card.
44. How old respondent was when received first library card.
45. How respondent acquired first library card.

Physical environment of the home

1. Other people who lived with family, including relationship to respondent, educational level, and period of time they lived with the family.
2. How many people respondent shared a bedroom with.
3. Where respondent studied.
4. Neatness and orderliness of the home (scale of 1 to 5).
5. Comparison of respondent's home to other homes in the community with respect to value and appearance (scale of 1 to 5).
*6. Presence of reading materials in the home (encyclopedia, dictionary, magazines subscriptions, daily newspaper, books, other than textbooks or cookbooks/manuals).
*7. Language of reading materials.

School/College characteristics

*1. Age at school entry.
2. Initial feelings about school.
3. When respondent first felt positive about school.
*4. Did respondent ever do poorly in school prior to college (grades of C or lower, behavior problems).
*5. Racial/ethnic composition of elementary school.
*6. Racial/ethnic composition of high school.
*7. Socio-economic composition of high school.
*8. Any teachers who were especially significant to the respondent either positively or negatively. In what way.
*9. Did respondent ever receive any special educational instruction (either remedial or advanced).
*10. Was respondent ever placed in a special classroom or "tracked" into a particular curriculum (including accelerated, remedial, bilingual, college prep, vocational, etc.)
*11. When respondent first began to get good grades (Bs or better).
*12. When respondent first remembered deciding to go to college.
*13. Impetus for graduate/professional education.
14. Did respondent ever experience conflict between continuing studies and helping family financially.
15. Did parents ever indicate a need for respondent to put aside studies to help family.
16. Was respondent a leader in elementary school (self-identified scale of 1 to 5).
17. Was respondent a leader in high school (self-identified scale of 1 to 5).
18. Was respondent "popular" in elementary school (self-identified scale of 1 to 5).
19. Was respondent "popular" in high school (self-identified scale of 1 to 5).
20. Did respondent belong to any clubs in high school.
21. Did respondent ever feel discriminated against because of ethnicity at any level of schooling.
*22. Did parents visit schools for any purpose (meetings, conferences, PTA, social functions), scale of 1 to 5.

Community characteristics

*1. Racial/ethnic composition of neighborhood(s) in which respondent grew up.
*2. Socio-economic composition of neighborhood(s) in which respondent grew up.

*3. Population density of neighborhood(s) (rural, urban, suburban)
4. Language(s) spoken in the neighborhood.
5. Estimated percentage of peers from the neighborhood who went on to college.
6. Estimated percentage of peers from school who went on to college.
7. Family's relative status in neighborhood (scale of 1 to 5).

Peer relations

1. Friendship groupings in elementary school (many friends; a few friends; loner).
2. Friendship groupings in high school (many friends; a few friends; loner).
3. Did respondent consider self "different" from peers. In what ways.
4. Characterization of friendship group at school (e.g., rowdy, studious, jocks, popular, average, gangmembers).
*5. Ethnicity of friends in high school.
*6. Ethnicity of friends in college.
*7. Clubs or organizations to which respondent belonged in college.
8. Was respondent admired for any special ability.
9. Did respondent have a special disability that interfered with peer relations.

Health

1. Did respondent ever have any particular health problem or physical disability that affected their schooling or peer relations.

Mexican American identity

1. How did parents feel about being Mexican or Mexican American. How did they characterize this.
2. Was respondent ever aware of discrimination against any family members. How was this handled.
3. How did each parent feel about Anglos.
4. Did parents have Anglo friends.
5. Did parents indicate their feelings about inter-ethnic dating, marriage, or friendships.
6. Did respondent ever experience discrimination because of ethnicity.
7. Was being Mexican American related in any way to academic success.
8. Does respondent think he/she looks "typically" Chicano.

9. Has respondent ever been mistaken for something other than Mexican American.
*10. Interviewer's assessment of skin color (scale of 1 to 3).
*11. Interviewer's assessment of phenotype (scale of 1 to 3).
12. Did respondent ever feel he/she had to "adopt" Anglo values to survive academically. Kinds of values.
13. Has respondent ever had to reject familial/cultural values to survive academically. Kinds of values.
14. Has respondent ever wished he/she weren't Mexican American.
15. Does respondent characterize family's value system as "typical" or "atypical" of other Mexican families. In what ways.
16. Does respondent feel that physical appearance has been a factor in school success. In what ways.

Attitudes and personality characteristics

*1. Personal characteristics possessed by respondent that were instrumental in school success.
2. Differences in respondent's background and experiences that distinguish him/her from less academically successful Mexican Americans.
*3. The single "critical variable" in respondent's academic success (internally or externally locused).
*4. Significant events that played a vital role in academic success (including opportunities offered).

Questions added to Sample II Women interview

1. Quality of elementary and high school education (scale of 1 to 5).
2. To what degree did feelings of competitiveness with peers motivate academic performance.
3. Did subject feel prepared for the college experience.
4. How did peer networks function to support college education.
5. Would subject's career path have been different if she weren't a woman.
6. Would subject's career path have been different without financial aid.

Bibliography

Aguirre, A., & Martinez, R. (1993). *Chicanos in higher education: Issues for the 21st century*. Washington, D.C.: The ERIC Clearinghouse on Higher Education and Association for the Study of Higher Education (ASHE). Report No.3.

Anderson, J., & Evans, F. (1976). Family socialization and educational achievement in two cultures: Mexican American and Anglo American. *Sociometry, 39*, 209–222.

Arce, C., Murguia, E., & Frisbie, W. P. (1987). Phenotype and life chances among Chicanos. *Hispanic Journal of Behavioral Science, 9*, 19–32.

Astin, A. W. (1982). *Minorities in American higher education*. San Francisco: Jossey–Bass.

Atkinson, J. W., & Feather, N. (Eds.) (1966). *A theory of achievement motivation*. New York: Wiley.

Averch, H. A., Carroll, S. J., Donaldson, T. S., Kiesling, H. J., & Pincus, J. (1974). *How effective is schooling?* Englewood Cliffs, New Jersey: Educational Technology.

Bandura, A. (1990). Conclusion: Reflections on nonability determinants of competence. In R. Sternberg and J. Kolligian, Jr. (Eds.), *Competence Considered*. New Haven: Yale University Press, 315–362.

Baumrind, D. (1989). Rearing competent children. In W. Damon (Ed.), *Child development today and tomorrow*. San Francisco: Jossey-Bass, 349–378.

Benard, B. (1991). *Fostering resiliency in kids: Protective factors in the family, school and community*. Portland, Oregon: Northwest Regional Educational Laboratory.

Bloom, B. (1985). *Developing talent in young people*. New York: Ballantine.

Bloom, G. (1991). *The effects of speech style and skin color on bilingual teaching candidates' and bilingual teachers' attitudes toward Mexican American pupils*. Unpublished doctoral dissertation, Stanford University.

Bourdieu, P., & Passeron, J. C. (1977). *Reproduction in education, society and culture.* Beverly Hills: Sage Publications.

Bowles, S., & Gintis, H. (1976). *Schooling in capitalist America.* New York: Basic Books.

Bryk, A., Lee, V., & Holland, P. (1993). *Catholic Schools and the common good.* Cambridge, Mass.: Harvard University Press.

Buenning, M., & Tollefson, N. (1987). The cultural gap hypothesis as an explanation for the achievement patterns of Mexican–American students. *Psychology in the Schools, 24,* 264–272.

California Postsecondary Education Commission (CPEC). (1986). *Enrollment trends in California higher education.* Sacramento: CPEC.

————. (1988). *The eleventh in a series of reports on new freshman enrollments at California's colleges and universities by recent graduates of California High Schools.* Sacramento: CPEC.

————. (1990). *Shortenting the time to the doctoral degree.* Sacramento: CPEC.

————. (1993). Unpublished data on 1992 graduate student enrollment by race, ethnicity, gender and discipline. Sacramento: CPEC.

California State Department of Education (CSDE). (1991). *Fingertip facts on education in California.* Sacramento: CSDE.

Caplan, N., Choy, M., & Whitmore, J. (1992, February). Indochinese refugee families and academic achievement. *Scientific American.* 36–42.

Carter, D., & Wilson, R. (1991). *Ninth annual status report on minorities in higher education.* Washington, D.C.: American Council on Education, Office of Minorities in Higher Education.

————. (1993). *Eleventh annual status report on minorities in higher education.* Washington, D.C.: American Council on Education, Office of Minorities in Higher Education.

Carter, T. (1970). *Mexican Americans in school.* New York: College Entrance Examination Board.

Carter, T., & Segura, R. (1979). *Mexican Americans in school: Decade of change.* New York: College Entrance Examination Board.

Castle, E. (1993). Minority student attrition research: Higher education's challenge for human resource development. *Educational Researcher, 22,* 24–30.

Chapa, J. (1991). Special focus: Hispanic demographic and educational trends. In D. Carter and R. Wilson, *Ninth annual status report on minorities in higher education.* Washington, D.C.: American Council on Education, 11–17.

Chapa, J., & Valencia, R. (1993). Latino population growth, demographic characteristics, and educational stagnation: An examination of recent trends, *Hispanic Journal of Behavioral Science, 15,* 165–187.

Cicourel, A., & Mehan, H. (1985). Universal development, stratifying practices, and status attainment. *Research in Social Stratification and Mobility, 4,* 3–27.

Clark, R. (1983). *Family life and school achievement: Why poor black children succeed and fail.* Chicago: University of Chicago Press.

Clayton, K., Garcia, G., Underwood, R., McEndree, P., & Shepherd, R. (1992). *The role of the family in the educational and occupational decisions made by Mexican American students.* Berkeley: National Center for Research on Vocational Education, University of California.

Coleman, J. (1961). *The adolescent society.* New York: The Free Press.

———. (1987). Families and schools. *Educational Researcher, 16,* 32–38.

Coleman, J., Campbell, E., Hobson, C., McPartland, J., Mood, A., Weinfield, F., & York, R. (1966). *Equality of educational opportunity.* Washington, D.C.: U.S. Government Printing Office.

Coleman, J., & Hoffer, T. (1987). *Public and private high schools: The impact of communities.* New York: Basic Books.

Coles, R. (1989). *The call of stories.* Boston: Houghton–Mifflin.

Comer, J. (1988). Educating poor minority children, *Scientific American, 259,* 42–48.

Cooney, R. (1975). Changing labor force participation of Mexican American wives: A comparison with Anglos and Blacks. *Social Science Quarterly, 56,* 252–261.

Cummins, J. (1981). The role of primary language development in promoting educational success for language minority students. In California State Department of Education, *Schooling and language minority students: A theoretical framework.* Los Angeles: Evaluation, Dissemination and Assessment Center, California State University.

———. (1986). Empowering minority students: a framework for intervention. *Harvard Educational Review, 56,* 18–36.

D'Amico, S. (1975). The effects of clique membership upon academic achievement, *Adolescence, 10,* 93–100.

Darcy, N. T. (1953). A review of the literature on the effects of bilingualism on the measurement of intelligence. *Journal of Genetic Psychology, 82,* 21–57.

Davé, R. (1964). *The identification and measurement of environmental process variables that are related to educational achievement.* Unpublished doctoral dissertation, University of Chicago.

De La Rosa, D., & Maw, C. (1990). *Hispanic education: a statistical report.* Washington, D.C.: National Council of La Raza.

Delgado–Gaitan, C. (1990). *Literacy for empowerment: The role of parents in children's education.* London: Falmer Press.

————. (1991). Involving parents in the schools: A process of empowerment. *American Journal of Education,* 100, 20–46.

DiMaggio, P. (1982). Cultural capital and school success: the impact of status culture participation on the grades of U.S. high school students. *American Sociological Review,* 47, 189–201.

Donato, R., Menchaca, M., & Valencia, R. (1991). Segregation, desegregation and integration of Chicano students: Problems and prospects. In R. Valencia (Ed.), *Chicano school failure and success.* New York: Falmer Press, 27–63.

Duran, B., & Weffer, R. (1992). Immigrants' aspirations, high school process, and academic outcomes. *American Educational Research Journal,* 29, 163–181.

Durán, R. (1983). *Hispanics education and background: Predictors of college achievement.* New York: College Entrance Examination Board.

Durán, R., Enright, M., & Rock. D. (1985). *Language factors and Hispanic freshmen's student profile.* Report No. 85–3. New York: College Entrance Examination Board.

Educational Testing Service (ETS). (1991). *The State of inequality.* Princeton, N.J.: ETS.

Epstein, J., & Karweit, N. (1983). *Friends in school: Patterns of selection and influence in secondary schools.* New York: Academic Press.

Erickson, F. (1987). Transformation and school success: The politics and culture of educational achievement. *Anthropology and Education Quarterly,* 18, 335–356.

Fernández, R. M., & Nielsen, F. (1986). Bilingualism and Hispanic scholastic achievement: Some baseline results. *Social Science Research,* 15, 43–70.

Fordham, S., & Ogbu, J. (1986). Black students' school success: Coping with the burden of "acting white." *Urban Review,* 18, 176–206.

Gage, W. L., & Berliner, D. (1991). *Educational Psychology.* Princeton, New Jersey: Houghton–Mifflin.

Gándara, P. (1982). Passing through the eye of the needle: High–achieving Chicanas. *Hispanic Journal of Behavioral Sciences,* 4(2), 167–179.

————. (1986a) Chicanos in higher education: The politics of self interest. *American Journal of Education,* 95, 256–272.

————. (1989). Those children are ours: Moving toward community. *Equity and Choice,* 5, 5–12.

————. (1992). Language and ethnicity as factors in school failure: The case of Mexican Americans. In R. Wollons (Ed.), *Children at risk in America.* New York: State University of New York Press.

Gandara, P. & Sun, A. (1986) *Bilingual Education: Learning English in California.* Sacramento: Assembly Office of Research.

Garmezy, N. (1974). Children at risk: The search for the antecendents of schizophrenia. Part I, Conceptual modes and research methods. *Schizophrenia Bulletin,* 8, 14–90.

Gibson, M. (1987). The school performance of immigrant minorities: A comparative view. *Anthropology and Education Quarterly, 18,* 262–275.

————. (1988). *Accommodation without assimilation: Sikh immigrants in an American high school.* New York: Cornell University Press.

————. (1993). Variability in immigrant students' school performance: The U.S. case. *Division G Newsletter,* Winter. Washington, D.C: American Educational Research Association.

Giroux, H. (1983). *Theory and resistance: A pedagogy for the opposition.* South Hadley, Massachusetts: Bergin and Garvey.

Glazer, N., & Moynihan, D. (1963). *Beyond the melting pot.* Cambridge: MIT Press.

Goertzel, M. G., Goertzel, V., & Goertzel, T. G. (1978). *Three hundred eminent personalities.* San Francisco: Jossey–Bass.

Goodman, Y., & Goodman, K. (1990). Vygotsky in a whole language perspective. In L. Moll (Ed.), *Vygotsky and education.* New York: Cambridge University Press.

Grebler, L., Moore, J., & Guzmán, R. (1970). *The Mexican–American people: The nation's second largest minority.* New York: Free Press.

Gutek, B. (1978). On the accuracy of retrospective attitudinal data. *Public Opinion Quarterly, 42,* 390–401.

Haaga, J. (1986). *Accuracy of retrospective data from the Malaysian family life survey.* Santa Monica, California: The Rand Corporation.

Hanushek, E. (1981). Throwing money at schools. *Journal of Policy Analysis, 1,* 19–41.

————. (1989). The impact of differential expenditures on school performance. *Educational Researcher, 18,* 45–51.

Henderson, R. (1966). *Environmental stimulation and intellectual development of Mexican American children.* Unpublished doctoral dissertation, University of Arizona, Tucson.

Henry, D. (1975). *Challenges past, challenges present: An analysis of American higher education since 1930.* San Francisco: Jossey–Bass.

Hess, R., & Shipman, V. (1965). Early experience and the socialization of cognitive modes in children. *Child Development, 36,* 869–886.

Hetherington, M. (1981). *Cognitive performance, school behavior, and achievement of children from one-parent households.* Washington, D.C.: National Institute of Education.

Holland, D., & Eisenhart, M. (1990). *Educated in romance: Women, achievement, and college culture.* Chicago: University of Chicago Press.

Hymes, D. (1974). *Foundations in sociolinguistics: An ethnographic approach.* Philadelphia: University of Pennsylvania Press.

Jacobi, M. (1991). Mentoring and undergraduate academic success: A literature review. *Review of Educational Research, 61,* 505–532.

Jencks, C., & Mayer, S. (1990). The social consequences of growing up in a poor neighborhood. In L. Lynee & M. McGeary (Eds.), *Innercity poverty in the United States.* Washington, D.C.: National Academy Press, 111–186.

Jencks, C., Smith, M., Acland, H., Bane, M. J., Cohen, D., Gintis, H., Heynes, B., & Mickelson, R. (1972). *Inequality.* New York: Harper & Row.

Karabel, J. (1981). *The politics of federal higher education policymaking: 1945–1980.* Report from the Project on Politics and Inequality in American Higher Education. Huron Institute. ERIC No. 223 171.

Laosa, L. (1978). Maternal teaching strategies in Chicano families of varied educational and socioeconomic levels. *Child Development, 49,* 1129–1135.

Laosa, L., & Henderson, R. (1991). Cognitive socialization and competence: The academic development of Chicanos. In R. Valencia (Ed.), *Chicano School Failure and Success.* London: Falmer Press, 165–199.

Lareau, A. (1987). Social class differences in family–school relationships: The importance of cultural capital. *Sociology of Education, 60,* 73–85.

————. (1989). *Home advantage: Social class and parental intervention in elementary education.* London, New York: Falmer Press.

Levine, D., Mitchell, E., & Havighurst, R. (1970). *Family status, type of high school and college attendance.* Kansas City: Center for the Study of Metropolitan Problems in Education.

LeVine, R. (1974). Parental goals: A cross cultural view. *Teacher's College Record, 76,* 227–239.

Lewis, O. (1961). *The children of Sanchez.* New York: Random House.

Lucas, T., Henze, R., & Donato, R. (1990). Promoting the success of Latino language–minority students: An exploratory study of six high schools. *Harvard Educational Review, 60,* 315–340.

Macías, R. (1993). Language and ethnic classification of language minorities: Chicano and Latino students in the 1990's, *Hispanic Journal of Behavioral Science, 15,* 230–257.

Marjoribanks, K. (1972). Ethnic and environmental influences on mental abilities. *American Journal of Sociology, 78,* 323–337.

————. (1988). Sibling, family environment and ability correlates of adolescents' aspirations: Ethnic group differences, *Journal of Biosocial Science, 20*, 203–209.

————. (1990). Sibling variable correlates of children's academic achievement: Family–group differences, *Psychological Reports, 67*, 147–154.

Matute-Bianchi, M. E. (1986). Ethnic identities and patterns of school success and failure among Mexican–descent and Japanese American students in a California high school. *American Journal of Education, 95*, 233–255.

McCarthy, K., & Valdez, R. B. (1986). *Current and future effects of Mexican immigrants in California.* Santa Monica: Rand Corporation R–3365–CR.

McClelland, D. (1965). Toward a theory of motive acquisition. *American Psychologist, 20*, 321–333.

McClelland, D., Atkinson, J., Clark, L., & Lowell, E. (1953). *The achievement motive.* New York: John Wiley & Sons.

McLaren, P. (1994). *Life in schools: An introduction to critical pedagogy in the foundations of education.* 2nd ed. New York: Longman.

McLeod, J. (1987). *Ain't no making it: Leveled aspirations in a low-income neighborhood.* Boulder, Colorado: Westview Press.

Mehan, H. (1992). Understanding inequality in schools: The contribution of interpretive studies. *Sociology of Education, 65*, 1–20.

Mehan, H., Hartweck, A., & Miehls, J. L. (1986). *Handicapping the handicapped.* Palo Alto: Stanford University Press.

Mehan, H., Hubbard, L., & Villanueva, I. (1994). Forming academic identities: Accommodation without assimilation among involuntary minorities. *Anthropology and Education Quarterly, 25*, 91–117.

Menneer, P. (1978). Retrospective data in survey research. *Journal of Market Research Society, 20*, 182–195.

Merino, B. (1991). Promoting school success for Chicanos: The view from inside the bilingual classroom. In R. Valencia (Ed.), *Chicano school failure and success.* New York: Falmer Press, 119–149.

Mittelbach, F., & Marshall, G. (1966). *The burden of poverty.* Advance report 5. Mexican American Study Project. Los Angeles: University of California.

Moles, O. (1982). Synthesis of research on parent participation in children's education. *Educational Leadership, 40*, 44–47.

Moll, L., & Vélez–Ibañez, C. (1992). Funds of knowledge for teaching: Using a qualitative approach to connect homes and classrooms. *Theory into Practice, 31*, 132–141.

Mortimore, P., Sammons, P., Stoll, L., Ecob, R., & Lewis, D. (1988). The effects of school membership on pupils' educational outcomes. *Research Papers in Education, 3,* 3–26.

Mulkey, L. (1992). One parent households and achievement: Economic and behavioral explanations of a small effect. *Sociology of Education, 65,* 48–65.

Muskal, F., & Carlquist, K. (1992). Getting there: Mentoring, mobility and social class. Unpublished paper. Stockton, California: University of the Pacific.

National Center for Education Statistics (1991). *Digest of education statistics.* Washington, D.C.: U. S. Department of Education.

Nieto, S. (1993). Linguistic diversity in multicultural classrooms. In H. S. Shapiro and D. Purpel (Eds.), *Critical social issues in American education: toward the 21st century.* White Plains, N.Y.: Longman, 194–211.

Oakes, J. (1985). *Keeping track: How schools structure inequality.* New Haven: Yale University Press.

Ogbu, J. (1987). Variability in minority school performance: A problem in search of an explanation. *Anthropology and Education Quarterly, 18,* 312–334.

Ogbu, J., & Matute-Bianchi, G. (1986). Understanding sociocultural factors: Knowledge identity and school adjustment. In *Beyond language: Social and cultural factors in schooling language minority students.* Los Angeles: Evaluation, Dissemination and Assessment Center, California State University, Los Angeles.

Olson, K. (1974). *The G.I. Bill, the Veterans, and the Colleges.* Lexington: University Press of Kentucky.

Orfield, G. (1990). Public policy and college opportunity. *American Journal of Education, 98*(4), 317–350.

Orfield, G., Montford, F., & George, P. (1987). *School desegregation in the 1980's: trends in the metropolitan areas.* National School Desegregation Project. Chicago: University of Chicago.

Orfield, G., & Paul, F. (1988). Declines in minority access: A tale of five cities. *Educational Record, 68*(4), 56–62.

Pincus, C., Elliott, L., & Schlachter, T. (1981). *The Roots of Success.* Englewood Cliffs, New Jersey: Prentice–Hall.

Policy Analysis for California Education (PACE). (1991). *The Condition of Education in California, 1990.* Berkeley: PACE.

Portes, A., & Rumbaut, R. (1993). *The assimilation process of children of immigrants.* Release No. 1 of The Children of Immigrants Project. Baltimore: Johns Hopkins University.

————. (1994). *The educational progress of children of immigrants.* Release No. 2 of The Children of Immigrants Project. Baltimore: Johns Hopkins University.

Portes, A., & Zhou, M. (1993). The new second generation: Segmented assimilation and its variants. *Annals, AAPSS, 530,* 75–96.

Post, D. (1990). College-going decisions by Chicanos: The politics of misinformation. *Educational Evaluation and Policy Analysis, 12,* 174–187.

Purkey, S., & Smith, M. (1983). Effective schools: A review. *The Elementary School Journal, 83,* 428–452.

Rendón, L., & Nora, A. (1989). A synthesis and application of research on Hispanic students in community colleges. *Community College Review, 17,* 17–24.

Rodriguez, R. (1982). *Hunger of memory.* New York: David R. Godine.

Rosenfeld, R. (1978). Women's intergenerational occupational mobility. *American Sociological Review, 43,* 36–46.

Rumberger, R. (1981). The rising incidence of over–education in the U.S. labor market. *Economics of Education Review, 1,* 291–314.

————. (1991). Chicano dropouts: A review of research and policy issues. In R. Valencia (Ed.), *Chicano school failure and success.* New York: Falmer Press, 64–89.

Rutter, M. (1979). Protective factors in children's responses to stress and disadvantage. In N. Kent & J. Ray (Eds.), *Primary prevention of psychopathology. Vol 3.: Social Competence in Children.* Hanover, New Hampshire: University Press of New England, 49–74.

Ryan, J., & Sackrey, C. (1984) *Strangers in paradise: Academics from the working class.* Boston: South End Press.

Schlossman, S. (1983). Is there an American tradition of bilingual education? Germans in the twentieth century public elementary schools. *American Journal of Education, 92,* 139–184.

Simonton, D. K. (1987). Developmental antecedents of achieved imminence. *Annals of Child Development, 4,* 131–169.

————. (1994). *Greatness: Who makes history and why.* New York: Guilford.

So, A. (1987). High–achieving disadvantaged students: A study of low SES Hispanic language minority youth. *Urban Education, 22*(1), 19–35.

Steelman, L. C. (1985). A tale of two variables: A review of the intellectual consequences of sibling size and birth order. *Review of Educational Research, 55,* 353–386.

Steinberg, L., Brown, B., Cider, M., Kaczmarck, N., & Lazzaro, C. (1988). *Noninstructional influences on high school student achievement: The contributions of parents, peers, extracurricular activities, and part–time work.* Madison, Wisconsin: National Center on Effective Secondary Schools.

Steinberg, L., Dornbusch, S., & Brown, B. (1992). Ethnic differences in adolescent achievement: And ecological perspective. *American Psychologist, 47*, 723–729.

Stevenson, D., & Baker, D. (1987). The family–school relation and the child's school performance. *Child Development, 58*, 1348–1357.

Stevenson, H., & Stigler, J. (1992). *The learning gap*. New York: Summit Books.

Stone, E. (1988). *Black sheep and kissing cousins: How our family stories shape us*. New York: Times Books.

Suárez–Orozco, M. (1987). Becoming somebody: Central American immigrants in U.S. inner–city schools. *Anthropology and Education Quarterly, 18*, 287–299.

Swartz, D. (1977). Pierre Bourdieu: The cultural transmission of social inequality. *Harvard Educational Review, 47*, 545–555.

Telles, E., & Murguía, E. (1990). Phenotypic discrimination and income differences among Mexican Americans. *Social Science Quarterly, 71*, 682–696.

Trueba, H. (1988). Culturally based explanations of minority students' educational achievement. *Anthropology and Education Quarterly, 19*, 270–287.

U.S. Department of Labor (1977; 1991). *Dictionary of occupation titles*. Washington, DC: U.S. Government Printing Office.

Valencia, R. (1991). The plight of Chicano students: An overview of schooling conditions and outcomes. In R. Valencia (Ed.), *Chicano school failure and success*. New York: Falmer Press, 3–26.

Valencia, R., Henderson, R., & Rankin, R. (1981). Relationship of family constellation and schooling to intellectual performance of Mexican American children. *Journal of Educational Psychology, 73*, 524–532

Valentine, C. (1968). *Culture and poverty: Critique and counter proposals*. Chicago: University of Chicago Press.

Wang, M., Haertel, G., & Walberg, H. (1994). Educational resilience in inner cities. In M. Wang & E. Gordon (Eds.), *Educational resilience in inner city America*. Hillsdale, New Jersey: Lawrence Erlbaum, 45–72.

Weinberg, S. K. (1994). Where the streets cross the classroom: A study of Latino students' perspectives on cultural identity in city schools and neighborhood gangs. Paper presented at the Language Minority Research Institute Conference, October 21–23, University of California, Riverside.

Weiner, B. (1980). *Human motivation*. New York: Holt, Rinehart & Winston.

Werner, E., & Smith, R. (1989). *Vulnerable but invincible: A longitudinal study of resilient children and youth*. New York: Adams, Bannister & Cox.

Willis, P. (1977). *Learning to labor: How working class kids get working class jobs.* New York: Columbia University Press.

Winkler, D. (1975). Educational achievement and school peer group composition. *Journal of Human Resources, 10,* 189–204.

Wolf, R. (1963). *The identification and measurement of environmental process variables related to intelligence.* Unpublished doctoral dissertation, University of Chicago.

Zajonc, R. B. (1976). Family configuration and intelligence. *Science, 192,* 227–416.

Index